Ceremonies Customs and Colour

Behind the
VEIL

Karachi
OXFORD   UNIVERSITY   PRESS
Oxford   New York   Delhi
1992

Ceremonies Customs and Colour

Behind the
VEIL

Shaista Suhrawardy Ikramullah

Oxford University Press, Walton Street, Oxford OX2 6DP

Oxford New York Toronto
Delhi Bombay Calcutta Madras Karachi
Kuala Lumpur Singapore Hong Kong Tokyo
Nairobi Dar es Salaam Cape Town
Melbourne Auckland Madrid
and associated companies in
Berlin Ibadan

Oxford is a trade mark of Oxford University Press

© Oxford University Press

First Published by Pakistan Publications, 1953

This Edition by Oxford University Press, 1992

ISBN 0 19 577419 1

Designed by
Creative Unit Private Ltd.
Printed in Pakistan by
Rosette Printers, Karachi.

Published in Pakistan by
Oxford University Press
5-Bangalore Town, Sharae Faisal,
P.O. Box 13033, Karachi-75350, Pakistan.

To my Mother
with whose
memory are
associated
my days
BEHIND
THE
VEIL

Foreword

uslim culture, as it shaped itself in the territories that once formed the Moghul empire of India, is a fascinating subject of study, having varied dimensions, to which full justice has not yet been done. Those accounts that have been written of it have been concerned more with the religious and spiritual aspects of it, dealing with it in the broader context of Islamic culture. There are several tiers of a cultural edifice, going up to the lofty, intellectual or imaginative spheres on the one hand, and descending to matters more mundane and down to earth, such as social habits, manners, myths, idiosyncrasies, rites and rituals, totems, taboos, etc., on the other. Abdul Haleem Sharar's celebrated work, *The Last Phase of an Oriental Culture*, which has been translated into English by E S Harcourt and Fakhir Husain, does indeed embrace a good deal more than do other formal, academic studies. He has dealt with arts and crafts, sports and pastimes, combat and weaponry, besides letters and learning, as they flourished in the feudal

environs of Lucknow, and, in a way, epitomized Indo-Muslim culture. But the picture he paints are peopled exclusively by men. One gains no acquaintance with the other half of the society — the half that lived behind the veil.

It is my belief that women are the true custodians of a people's culture, nurturing not only its peripheral aspects, but also the faiths and beliefs which form the core of culture. It is women who transmit the myths, the folklore, the ethnic biases and *esprit de corp* of a people from generation to generation. The individual holds tenaciously to the faith taught him by his mother, and cannot easily be weaned away from it. Women are also more conservative than men. This remark, I think, needs no apology, being more likely to be taken as a compliment by our women. It is also backed by socio-psychological observation. Traditions mean more to women and are safer in their hands.

Begum Shaista Ikramullah has, for the first time, afforded the English reader what is more than just a peep behind the veil. She takes us into all the nooks and corners of the *harem* or, more aptly, the *haveli* and makes a whole pageant of colourful ceremonies pass before our eyes. We are for a while lost in the glamour of it all. She lays before us a wide perspective of life as it was lived for generations in female society, and which has not yet totally passed into oblivion. The culture she depicts flourished mainly in the urban Muslim society of the Indo-Gangetic plains, stretching from Delhi, where it took root, to Murshidabad and beyond. Vestiges of it have trailed down to our times, both in India and Pakistan. Though the feudal order still flourishes in this country, the culture associated with it has its own native stamp. It does, however, share some features with the Muslim culture of the subcontinent, in the broader sense.

The present work also gives us glimpses of the local culture, such as bridal dresses and decorations that are patently Pakistani.

With the gradual lifting of the veil, and the growth of mixed societies, male and female behaviour, which erstwhile had definite distinctions — which were reflected even in the manner of speech — now tends to show similarities. The ladies of Delhi and Lucknow employed their own peculiar idiom and vocabulary, which was very charming to male ears. Even now, though the distinction has all but vanished, the patently female exclamation *ooi* will never slip from the mouth of a man, or even a very young boy.

The characters we meet in this book are, of course, types lacking individuality, for the obvious reason that the author set out to write neither memoirs nor fiction but was recording her observations and experiences in an epitomized form. But the descriptions do have dramatic touches without a conscious attempt at dramatization.

This is the second edition of the book which first appeared in 1953. Begum Ikramullah has revised it slightly here and there, besides adding some more pictorial material and an additional chapter. It is one of several notable works that have come from her pen. Her first scholarly work was a thesis that she did for her Ph.D., on the development of the Urdu novel. Incidentally she was the first Muslim woman to have obtained a doctorate in Urdu from the

London University. In her later career she also briefly entered politics as a supporter of the Pakistan movement, and was a member of Pakistan's first Constituent-cum-Legislative Assembly. Her early life was spent in an orthodox environment. She has given us an interesting account of her emergence from it in her reminiscences entitled *From Purdah to Parliament*. In another work, *Letters to Neena,* she sets out the case for Pakistan, and the partition of India, in a style familiar to an Indian reader. It would be difficult to name another instance of a stand being taken on a heated controversy — in the present case, one that shook and split a subcontinent — in the form of personal letters that are full of warmth, but skilfully synchronized with cold reasoning. With her affable manners and intellectual gifts, she was well fitted to be an ambassador, and did actually represent Pakistan in Morrocco for a few years. She was the wife of Mr M Ikramullah, a diplomat, who was Pakistan's first Foreign Secretary.

Begum Ikramullah's latest work, prior to the present —also published by Oxford University Press, Pakistan — is an intimate biographical sketch of Huseyn Shaheed Suhrawardy, a colourful political personality of his times, and an ex-Prime Minister of Pakistan. Her works, including the present book, are indeed valuable contributions to the political and social studies of our people and our times. No one could have done better justice to the subjects she has undertaken in trying out her unmistakable talent for penmanship.

Shanul Haq Haqee   Karachi,
                                         July 1991.

Introduction to the
Second Edition

s I said in my first Introduction to *Behind the Veil*, I wrote the essays that comprise it for my Western friends. These were not written with the intention of their being published in a book form. That came about incidentally.

The creation of Pakistan, which at that time was the first and the largest Muslim State to have achieved independence, generated a great deal of interest and there was much curiosity about it in the West, especially since it had once been part of the subcontinent of India. It was mainly the Westerners who were keen to know what the reasons were for the need for a separate state, and eventually, for the creation of it.

A stream of visitors poured into Pakistan. Miss Fatima Jinnah would say to me, 'Take them out and tell them about Pakistan.'

I did just that, I told them about the reasons for the creation of Pakistan. I told them about the magnitude of its political problems; of the refugees and their plight; but at the same time, I also gave them a glimpse of our way of life. I took them to lunches and to teas, and told them about Pakistan. I showed them houses which had some vestige left of our way of life, and showed them whatever of our culture and treasures remained — the trousseaus of the brides of the *taluqdars* of Lucknow, jewels from princely states whose members had taken refuge in Pakistan. 'This is nothing, we've lost practically everything,' would be my comment, as I took our stacks of saris and *joras* from almirahs and boxes.

Perhaps I was overdoing it!

'It beats me to think what you were like if this is what you have left after having lost most of it,' said an American friend, to whom I was showing *tulwan joras* after *tulwan joras* of Suraya, daughter of the Raja of Nanpara, with the comment, 'This is nothing. In Rampur, the brides of Rampur could barely stand up in their *chauthi ka jora*.'

If there was a wedding on, I took them to the ceremonial part of it, not to the Western-style reception, which was the only thing they were generally invited to at that time. I found that my Western visitors were fascinated, and more interested in customs followed 'behind the veil', than in politics. They asked me many questions as to the meaning and significance of these customs, and I tried my best to answer them. I began making notes, and before I realized it they had turned into essays. I took these to show to Miss Jinnah. She glanced at them, and said, 'Yes, they are quite interesting. I think it would be a good idea to bring out a magazine for women with essays such as these.'

I agreed. Miss Jinnah then asked me to go and see the Secretary of the Information Department.

The Secretary of the Information Department at that time was Mian Arshad Hussain, the son of the great scholar, Mian Afzal Hussain, and son-in-law of the great educationist, Mian Fazl-i-Hussain, whose contribution towards the progress and education of the Muslims of the Punjab is well known; so it was natural that Mian Arshad Hussain would be sympathetic to the project.

We had more than one discussion, to decide matters such as whether the magazine should be a monthly or a quarterly one. He decided that it should be a quarterly, because that would enable it to achieve a higher standard of production; also it would be easier to get good articles every three months rather than every month. Mian Sahib said he would have to look into the finances and other necessary conditions before undertaking the launching of the project; he would begin doing so immediately and would let me know the result.

This was all within the first few months of Pakistan, before we knew that tragedy was to strike us. Quaid-i-Azam died — a bare thirteen months after the creation of Pakistan — all our shining dreams and grand schemes seemed to have been shattered!

The task of saving, and building, the nascent state of Pakistan absorbed everyone's energies. Luckily for us, led by Nawabzada Liaquat Ali Khan, we had at that time a group of people who rose to the occasion, and Pakistan survived.

Personally I was too shattered to even remember that I had some essays lying with the Information Department. One day, some three years or so later, when my husband was posted as High Commissioner for Pakistan in Canada, he brought from the Embassy a beautifully got up magazine, called the *Pakistan Quarterly*. It had some excellent articles, and beautiful photographs. In fact, it was very like the magazine that Mian Arshad Hussain and I had talked about bringing out, and in it, was one of the essays that I had left with Mian Arshad Hussain. At this stage I was rather pleased about it.

But when in the second and third issues of the *Quarterly* my essays kept coming out regularly without acknowledgement, I was annoyed, and wrote a stinker to the Information Department. I don't remember who the Secretary was then, but I did know that by that time Mian Arshad Hussain had joined the Foreign Service. Anyway, I gave his reference. I got a reply, acknowledging that my essays were with the Information Department. In fact, the Information Department was contemplating bringing them out in book form. This pleased me very much.

I provided two sets of wedding pictures, one of the wedding of the daughter of the First Agent General of Hyderabad, Deccan, which was celebrated with all the pomp and ceremonies of the past, and the other of the niece of Begum Abdul Qadir, whose husband had been one of the *Dewans* of Junagadh, so there was a *rayasti* flavour to it. Together with it there were some interesting ceremonies connected with Bombay, such as a tracery of flowers in the bridal chamber of which I had also got photographs.

I also had some photographs taken of things belonging to me, such as a *pandan*, a *khasdan*, an *itrdan*, a *gulabpash*, etc. From Canada I sent a photograph showing a bride surrounded by her friends (this was of an Embassy Secretary's wife, and my daughters, and of Nadira Masud and Anjum Chattari). I also added an essay showing that ladies behind the veil did not confine themselves only to fun and frivolity, but did a lot of social work, from their homes for their neighbourhood — work which is now done by women sitting on Committees.

It seemed that the Information Department was really thinking of bringing out the essays in book form, for the book arrived fairly soon, but I was very disappointed to see the poor quality of the production, and particularly the pictures. They had not used my pictures on ceremonies at all; there were not more than two or three pages of the pictures I had supplied of my personal things and there were none of the things mentioned above, and none of the dresses or ceremonies I had written about. The Information Department had collected the pictures and, while some of them were not bad, others did not portray in the least, what I had in mind. I was very upset and did not take much interest in the distribution of the book. As a publication of the Department of Information it was distributed by them I suppose. I was given a few copies which I gave to friends, apologizing for the pictures.

Soon after, I left Canada. I heard of some amusing incidents that the book had produced. There had been reviews of it in the Canadian papers, and when they heard that a child was born in the Pakistan Embassy, the Press wanted to come and see the ceremonies! There were none! Then there was a wedding in Washington. Again I was told that the Press came armed with a copy of *Behind the Veil* to see the various ceremonies. The modern young couple, who had not catered for this, were forced to have at least the *arsi-mushaf* — with a hand-mirror! There has now been a revival of the old customs and ceremonies with a vengeance, and when I critisize the vulgar ostentation of it all, my daughter Salma says, 'It is all your fault, people were happily forgetting the old customs and ceremonies. You, and your *Behind the Veil*, have revived it all.' I refuse to take the blame. The ceremonies nowadays are not performed at all as they were in times behind the veil. If they were, the *dulhan* sitting in *manjah*, would not be seen by any of her men relatives — much less have her fiance sitting and chatting to her, as I hear is done now. Anyway, it was all so long ago.

Years passed, and I had just one copy of the book left and this I lent to my dear friend Begum Jehanara Habibullah who comes from Rampur, India. She is the sister of the late Begum of Rampur and shares my love for the past and its gaiety and ceremonies which made life so interesting. She and I share memories and books about the past, and so I gave her my *Behind the Veil* to read. I was extremely surprised at her reaction. She was delighted with it, and felt that the book should be read by our girls. 'They know nothing about these customs and ceremonies,' Jehanara *behan* said.

'I don't think they are very interested', I replied.

'No they are,' she insisted, 'I gave it to my daughter and she mentioned the names of several other girls, all of whom seemed very interested and wanted to know from where they could get a copy.'

'It is out of print,' I said. 'They will not be able to get it anywhere.'

'Then you must get it printed again,' Jehanara *behan*

said. Just to please Jehanara *behan* and not to seem rude by rejecting her suggestion out of hand, I took the copy of *Behind the Veil* to show it to Mrs Ameena Saiyid, the General Manager of Oxford University Press, who had just published my book on my cousin, Huseyn Shaheed Suhrawardy. To my surprise, Ameena seemed to like the idea, and asked whether she could keep the book to read. I readily agreed.

On my next visit to OUP, Ameena said she had liked the book very much and wanted to bring out a second edition of it with the necessary corrections, etc. I could hardly believe my ears, but I was delighted, for I was sure that now at last it would be produced as I had wanted it to be, for in it is a faint reflection of the glory that was the Delhi of the Moghuls, and the granduer that was the Lucknow of the Nawabs of Oudh. In it is a reflection of the life of the Muslim aristocracy as it was lived before the decline set in. So this is how *Behind the Veil* was rescued from oblivion and has now been reprinted — entirely due to Jehanara *behan's* discernment, with which, luckily, Ameena Saiyid concurred, and Shanul Haq Haqqee Sahib, by agreeing to write a most appreciative foreword, has given it the stamp of authenticity.

Haqee Sahib's mentioning that ladies behind the veil had a distinctive vocabulary, of their own, reminded me, that I had forgotten to mention this. Ladies did have a style of speech all their own, and it was delightfully piquant, simple and chaste, not overburdened with Arabic or Persian words.

I immediately set about writing a chapter on this but it was too late as the book was already in the printing

stage.

For sometime now just for my own amusement I have been collecting *kahawats* and *mahavaras* as every sentence of a lady behind the veil was interspersed with a *kahawat* or a *mahavara*. May be I will have these printed separately, as yet another facet of life behind the veil.

Shaista S Ikramullah

Introduction to the
First Edition

his is a collection of essays written
from time to time for my Western
friends. I have called them *Behind the
Veil* because it was in the leisurely
and luxurious life behind the veil that
these customs originated, and even
today it is in the women's world that
they hold sway.

Our men have, by and large, adopted the western
dress, and in the sober hues they now wear there is
nothing left of the colourful East; but our women's
dresses still have, in their variety of style and
brightness of hue and richness of grace, all that is
associated with the Orient; and the dazzle of their
jewellery is reminiscent of the splendour of the
Moghul Courts. It is in the women's world,
unobserved and unattended by men, that the
numerous ceremonies take place. They are behind the
veil for the ordinary visiting foreigner, so he does not
see or even suspect that ceremonies almost medieval
in their picturesqueness still take place in the modern
city of Karachi, and that while attending them our
women shed their veneer of sophistication and revel

in all the pageantry of the East.

To give these foreigners a glimpse behind the veil, and to show them some of the richness and colourfulness of our way of life is the object of these articles.

In describing the customs and ceremonies, I have often wandered into the past, for it was the courts of the Moghul Kings of Delhi and Lucknow that set the fashion that is followed to this day. It was in that age of splendour and opulence, in that era of gracious living, that this manner of life was evolved. Not much of it has survived today, but as it took the better part of seven hundred years to build up this civilization it could not be destroyed in a century, even though that century had been one of cataclysmic social changes, following violent political upheavals. In 1857, the last vestige of the Moghul Court disappeared from Delhi, and with it went the way of life it had nurtured. With the disappearance of the grandees and nobles who had been associated with the King, wealth disappeared and, with it, the leisure that made such a life possible.

But, even in my childhood it was possible to meet people who had seen something of the vanished glory and who could tell the story of that past. I was particularly lucky in having met several people of this kind when I was a little child. There was a great-aunt of mine who died in 1929, at the age of eighty. This means that she was born just before the First War of Independence of 1857, so the fortunes of her family had not begun to decline till she was about nineteen. She not only remembered the past but had the power to reconstruct it. On cold winter nights she would collect us, the children of the family, under her soft, warm eiderdown and tell us of her childhood, and it seemed like a fairy tale. She had that priceless gift of a raconteur of telling a thing in the smallest detail. She would describe how *mehndi* was put on her finger, and the exact colour and trimmings of her *Eid* dress, in so vivid a manner that one almost saw it happening before one's eyes. From her I learned the names of the old pieces of jewellery. While those of our generation are content to call all ornaments for the hands 'bracelets', and all ornaments for the neck 'necklaces', she always gave each piece of jewellery its special name according to its style. She lived almost entirely in the past; that short period of her life when she was happy was more real to her than the long bleak years that followed, and she, therefore, made it real for her listeners also. She not only remembered, she lived in the past; her code of conduct, her behaviour, and her open-handed generosity, all belonged to a vanished age. From her, I learned much of the mode of life and the values that prevailed then.

There was another person who, in her own humble way, was a personification of the past. This was an old maid-servant of our family. She had begun life as a *laundi*, i.e., virtually a slave girl, in my great-grandfather's household, but had long ago reached such a position of respectability and honour that no one except the great-aunt I have mentioned above dared call her by her first name. She was intensely loyal and devoted to the family in which she had been brought up, and felt the change in their fortune more keenly than they themselves did. She had become a sort of custodian of family traditions; she was for ever reprimanding us girls and reminding us of our heritage. My own mother, and the mothers of my cousins, always sent for her and put her in charge of us girls whenever they went visiting. We disliked her greatly, but were mortally afraid of her and respected her, for she had a dignity of manner which many a lady of today might envy! It goes to prove more than anything else, how high the standard of the culture of the time was, which could produce maid-servants like her.

Much more popular with us than Husna *Bua* was another maid-servant called Lal Bibi, for she was virtually a walking volume of the *Arabian Nights*. She was a born storyteller and knew how to get the best response from her audience. She would never tell us a story while daylight lingered and, as she always left off her story every evening at the most critical stage, she kept us on tenterhooks for the whole of the next day. Even after dusk, she would not start the story straight away; she would take her time over her dinner, and then leisurely make herself a few *pans* and put them in a rusty tin box, and then sniff a little tobacco, while we hovered around her like chickens. Our impatience had no effect whatsoever on her. At last, she would seat herself comfortably on a low stool, take her favourite amongst the children on her knees, and begin the story. She would stop every now and then to take another *pan* or to have a sip of water, or even to run down to see if her grandchild was properly covered! In short, she did everything possible to whet our appetites. Lal Bibi came from Murshidabad and had seen much of the Nawabi regime in its decaying years, and her stories about real people were as interesting as the fiction she recounted.

Having thus got a taste for the past in my childhood, I followed it up when I, luckily, came to live in Delhi. *Lal Qila*, that seat of Moghul glory, had been a barrack and a museum for more than five decades, but it was not impossible to find a few who had seen the grandees who had once dwelt there, and who could tell the stories of the *Nawabzadas* who went riding on noble horses, and of the *Begums* who slept on flower bedecked beds.

Khawaja Hasan Nizami, whose books on the First War of Independence and its impact on Delhi are regarded as classics, had the power to make the Delhi of the past live again in his talks, as much as in his writings, and I have listened spellbound to his stories of the Delhi that was. Rashid-ul-Khairi was on his deathbed when I met him but among his family I found many who were the embodiment of the old Delhi culture itself. Hakim Ajmal Khan, the last of Delhi's great men, had just passed away, but his family continued the proud tradition of their illustrious forebears, and I was once privileged to see a wedding in their family. I had the good fortune of coming to know many people who retained the flavour of Delhi's traditions, and from their conversations I could piece together the colourful mosaic of the life of their past. I was priviliged to have met persons like Asif Ali Sahib and Khawaja Mohammad Shafi. To hear them talk and to hear the lilt of their Urdu was like listening to the cadance of music. Delhi, which had borne the brunt of repeated invasions and ravages of loot, had little left of wealth and prosperity, but in Lucknow there were still a number of *taluqdars*, i.e., families of the landed gentry, retaining some of their wealth. Consequently

they were able, to a greater extent, to keep up the
standard of living of their ancestors, while the States
of Rampur, Bhopal and Hyderabad were enclaves
where the colour and legendary romance of the past
were still preserved, and on ceremonial occasions
one got the impression of stepping right back into the
past. Even as late as 1941, the year I went to
Hyderabad, Deccan, the hours were proclaimed by a
naubat, and liveried retainers holding gold and silver
staffs flanked the entrance drive to the palaces of the
nobles, and one still sat down to a sixteen course
meal!

In Hyderabad, Deccan, there were still families who
could trace their descent from the nobles who had
come over with Asif Jah the First, the most
interesting among them being Nawab Salar Jang, in
whose family, for seven generations, had been vested
the Command of the Army. He himself was the last
of his line, a romantic and almost legendary figure,
who, symbolically, died a few weeks after the Indian
invasion of Hyderabad. And so passed this last
bastion of Moghul culture and, less brutally but as
effectively, were destroyed Bhopal, Rampur, and
myriads of other ancient Muslim and Hindu States.
For the Hindu States also, especially those of
Rajasthan, such as Jaipur and Jodhpur, had come
very much under the influence of the Moghuls, and
the etiquette that prevailed in their courts till
yesterday was that of the Moghul courts, while many
a colourful customs of the Rajputs had found their
way into the homes of the Muslim aristocracy.

The last cataclysmic upheaval that followed the
withdrawal of the British seemed to have sounded the
final death-knell to all this. In 1947 the streets of

Delhi once again ran with blood, and the oft-looted Muslim houses were looted and sacked once again, and refugees poured into the small new town of Karachi, then the proud capital of Pakistan. Jewels that had been handed down for generations, and silver that had been treasured for decades were all lost. It looked as if never again would one see in any household even a faint echo of the past grandeur. Yet, as the months passed and the wounds healed, phoenix-like the manners and customs of the past revived in this new State of Pakistan and *Eid, Baqr Eid, Shab-i-Barat, Ramadan, Rajab* and *Moharram* are all once again celebrated with the appropriate ceremonies. Though a child's education today does not follow the orthodox pattern, the ceremony of *Maktab* is still performed, and the finishing of the Quran is still considered necessary, despite all the preoccupations of the modern child with worldly sciences. The first attempt of a child to face the rigours of fasting is still rewarded by a party known as *roza kushai,* and the all-important wedding ceremony is today as much an occasion of fun and feasting and display of clothes and jewels as it ever was; and so the links with the past continue! Much has changed; there are today no houses in Karachi where there are separate women's apartments, and milady has had to make drastic reductions in her staff; but despite all this, much of the colour, much of the mystery of life behind the veil persists, even in the life of the most modern of us. I, for one, hope that it will be so for many a year to come, and that we shall, no matter how modern we become, never lose the magic and the colour that the words 'East' and 'Orient' bring to mind.

Interior of a Muslim Home

I

ift up the veil and let us enter the interior of a Muslim home! This would have been literally true a few decades ago, for women's apartments were completely separate from the men's. A long passage connected the two, and a heavy curtain hung at the end which gave entrance to the *Zenana*. There sat a female porter or *bara darni*, as she was called, and she announced the entry of all; even the menfolk of the family did not enter unannounced. The passage opened on to a courtyard flanked by rooms on all sides; in front of the rooms were verandahs — these were known as *dalans*. The largest was called the *sadr dalan* and was the equivalent of a drawing-room; the ones leading from it were known as *dalans* or *dar-dalans*. They were distinguished from each other as west *dalan*, east *dalan*, little *dalan*, etc. *Dalans* were really the living-rooms; though some were used for sleeping in the winter months; in the summer months, one always slept out in the courtyard. Then there were the small rooms known as *taha khanas*, used for

storing essentials. But one does not see houses of this style nowadays except in the older parts of the city in Lahore, Peshawar and Dhaka. In a modern city like Karachi, it would not be possible to find a single house of this type. In fact, at first glance, a Pakistani house or drawing-room in Karachi appears in no way different from a Western one, but a second glance would show some distinctive oriental touches in it. Together with all modern necessities, there will be seen pieces of furniture distinctly oriental in character. In the centre of the drawing-room will be a *takht*. In a large room there will be two or three *takhts* placed along the walls, one facing the entrance, the others on the sides. *Takhts* vary in size and are found in every Pakistani house. On the *takht*, there will be a *masnad*. The *masnad* is a heavily embossed or embroidered tapestry of the size 6' x 4' to anything up to 20' x 18', depending on the size of the *takht*. It is made of velvet embroidered with gold thread, satin embroidered with silk thread, or heavy woven tapestry. On the *masnad* will be found long bolsters for reclining, with two, or sometimes more, smaller bolsters on either side. The bolsters are generally embroidered to match the *masnad* in their material and style of embroidery. These are not put there as picturesque relics of the past but are the common mode of sitting in Pakistani houses.

On a low stool by the side of the *takht* or on the *masnad* itself, you invariably find a large silver casket known as the *pandan*. This is as typical of a Muslim home, as a box of cigarettes is in a western drawing-room. A *pandan* is a silver casket with several chambers which contain the ingredients that go to make *pan*, which is betel leaf. Betel plays the same part in our social life as cigarettes do in the western hemisphere, i.e., visitors or guests are generally offered *pans*. At parties, the passing of *pans* to each other signifies the same bonhomie which extending of cigarette cases does in the West. The *pans* are wrapped in silver paper known as *varaq* and are held together by means of silver pins or rings or put through silver foil circlets and served on silver or gold trays covered with dome-like structures, which are known as *khasdans*.

The other very special thing by the side of a *takht* used to be the *hooqah*, that was a pipe attached to a goblet, used for smoking. The cheaper and more portable cigarette has done away with the popularity of the *hooqah* and it no longer has a place of honour in every Muslim home as the *pandan* still has. *Hooqahs* usually had a base of silver or sometimes even of gold; brass, copper and steel were also used. These were beautifully carved, burnished or enamelled, and are still to be found in Muslim homes, serving as a base for lamps or vases or just as ornaments. From the base rose a long tube-like structure, and on this was kept a tray that held the embers. From the side of the base projected a spout which was either a straight pipe or a long coil which could be smoked while lying down or reclining, and which could be passed round quite a distance in the room. Before the advent of cigarettes, the *hooqah* was the favourite form of smoking and was handed to visitors with spout caps, known as *mohnals*, for their individual use. These spout caps were made of silver, jade, marble or gold.

Guests were welcomed on formal occasions by being presented with *itr*, i.e., scent, in embossed oriental

Above:
Greeting guests

Left:
Aftaba on a
chowki

caskets and, on grand occasions rose-water was sprinkled on them as well. Rose-water for this purpose was kept in silver bottles with long slender stems. These bottles were known as *gulab-pash*, or rose-water sprinklers. A set of *itrdan, gulab-pash, khasdan, hooqah, pandan* and *ugaldan* (spittoon) formed the essential pieces of the household silver, and were the first things bought for a bride when the dowry was prepared. An *ugaldan* is a spittoon and is a necessary corollary of the *pandan*. It is also usually of silver, or of some other metal, but always beautifully polished or engraved, and finds its place on the edge of the *masnad* in a typical oriental room; while the *gulab-pash* and *itrdan* are found on a bracket in a handy place in the room to be made available for welcoming guests and visitors.

Flowers are not only arranged in vases and put in niches in a room but are used in many other ways also. Garlands of flowers, as well as posies, are given to guests at formal parties. Flowers are strung and worn round the hair by girls and women, and no marriage is complete without a *sehra*, which is a lacelike veil of flowers worn by the bride and bridegroom. Photographs are not found in a typical Muslim home; instead of photographs, verses in beautiful calligraphy are framed and hung on the walls.

Before the days of the electric fan, there used to be suspended from the ceiling a sort of pendulant which was pulled by a string and thus gave a breeze. This style of fan also lent itself to a great deal of decoration and ingenuity. Hand fans are still used and are made in a great variety of styles and shapes: round, square, oval; they are made of velvet or satin

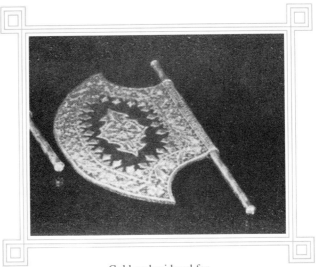

Gold-embroidered fan

Chilamchi

with silver handles, or are embroidered, and are
fitted with brightly coloured wooden handles. Ladies
of fashion take their fans and their *pans* wherever
they go. The *pans* are carried in small silver boxes.
These are beautifully made, and inside are still
smaller boxes which contain their favourite tobacco.
On a lady's dressing-table you would find, besides
the *itrdan*, a silver comb, a mirror with a silver
handle, several little silver boxes which would
contain gold powder and gold sequins, used for
decorating the hair; there would also be a silver oil
bottle for hair-oil. In the past, beds were made of
silver also, but nowadays very few people can afford
them; these beds were somewhat similar in style to
the old fashioned four-posters, with beautifully
carved legs and curtain-poles.

In the dinning-room, one did not use tables and
chairs in the Western way, but the room had two or
three *takhts* in a line and people sat around them on a
beautifully carpeted floor. The plates were of the
highest quality of china, and food was served in
copper, china, or glass bowls of various sizes. Our
dinner service is not very different from a Western
dinner service. We have the same sort of large and
small plates, and small bowls are used instead of the
entree dishes. Forks were not used at all, and spoons
only for serving; but if anyone thinks that eating with
your fingers just means plunging your hand into the
food, he is sorely mistaken. Eating with the fingers
has its code, and the well-brought up eat in such a
way that just the tips of the fingers are soiled. Still,
even for this, more adequate washing facilities than
the mere dipping of fingers in a bowl are necessary;
therefore, we have a *chilamchi* and *aftaba*, i.e., a

large bowl, and a goblet with a spout in the dinning-room. These are also made of silver, or any other metal, and are typical household articles. A servant holds the *aftaba* and pours water on to the hands for washing, and carries the soap and towel. The *chilamchi*, i.e., the receptacle into which the water is poured, has a perforated lid so one does not get splashed while washing one's hand.

Drinking water is kept in earthenware flasks known as *surahies,* or pitchers known as *gharas,* which are kept cool and moist by wrapping a wet cloth around them, keeping them in a cool room, and by putting them outside at night. In this way, water is more pleasantly cooled than in the crude way of icing it; a drop of *keora* is added to the water in summer. To keep the rooms cool, *khas* — a species of dry grass which exudes a refreshing fragrant smell, somewhat like hay when water is sprinkled on it — is put against the doors and windows. All through the long hot summer afternoons, servants sprinkle water on the *khas* to keep the rooms cool.

This way of living was indeed an expensive and elaborate one; but it had a great deal of charm and grace about it, and such a background could not but inculcate polished and elegant manners, but more of this in the next chapter.

Customs, Traditions and Etiquette

II

raditions and customs had evolved a framework of etiquette which was adhered to rigidly amongst us, the disregarding of which was frowned upon and considered a sign of ill-breeding. For instance, if one was paying someone a first, or otherwise formal visit, one always took a tray full of sweets, some dried or fresh fruits, or even a tray of each. This was done more particularly if one was visiting a house where there were children in the family. To visit a new neighbour for the first time, or to call on your would be daughter-in-law's family, or to visit a niece in her new house, and to omit to take sweets would certainly mark you out as mean or ill-bred and unaware of social niceties.

Even kind inquires from an older lady of high social status are accompanied by a tray of sweets, and the recipient of the sweets must, if she can, immediately replace it with similiar eatables, slightly varied, of course; e.g., if a tray full of *ladoos* has been brought, a tray full of *balu-shahis* ought to be returned. Except where a wedding is afoot, such an

immediate return of courtesies is not really
necessary, but a couple of rupees, or even a fiver, is
put on the tray for the servant who brings it.
Omission to do this will immediately dub you as 'no
lady' in the eyes of the maid-servant. In fact, to
know when, and how much, to tip is an important
part of a lady's education.

The departure of a friend or a relative from the house
calls for certain traditional observances by the lady of
the house. Before the person sets out on his journey,
sadqa is given. *Sadqa* is money which the person
going on the journey has touched, and it is
distributed and given in charity; this is supposed to
ward off any accidents or mishaps. The person
setting out on a journey is also made to look into a
bowl of clear mustard oil, and is made to sprinkle
some grains of *mash* in it. As he goes out of the
door, a copy of the Holy Quran is held over his head
and, of course, an *Imam Zamin* is always tied on his
arm. *Imám Zamins* are brought by everyone who
comes to say goodbye. Neglecting to do this would
really be a sign of gross ignorance. The *Imam Zamin*
is an armlet, beautifully embroidered and stitched,
with words such as 'Godspeed', 'God be your
Protector', etc., embroidered on it, and in it is
enclosed a rupee or two, or even a sovereign, to be
distributed to the poor after one's destination has
been safely reached. It is a formal token of goodbye,
like taking flowers when going to say goodbye to
someone in the West.

A visit of leave-taking is expected from anyone about
to go on a longish journey, and a visit on his return
is also one of the things done. These courtesies are
more particularly observed where relationships are

more formal in nature, or newly-formed such as those between two families recently related by marriage. For, at that time, a mental stock-taking is taking place and it is by such observances that it is decided whether or not you are of the elite!

One's friends are expected to call on occasions that demand congratulations or condolence, and an omission to do so is chalked against one. There are certain formalities that are observed even on a visit of condolence. In the past, one of the distinguishing things about a visit of condolence was that the transport was paid for by the visitor himself. On every other occasion the hostess always paid, but as visits these days have become far too frequent, this formality no longer holds. Other formalities are, however, still observed. For instance, for three days no fire is lit and no food is cooked in the house where there has been a death. Friends and relatives arrange to send food for the bereaved family; this is known as *hazri*.

The news of the safe return of someone, or any other success, or escape from a hazard, was promptly an occasion for *niaz*. These are sweets distributed in thanksgiving. A *niaz* could be given on the spur of the moment or promised earlier to one's favourite saint. On such occasions *gul-poshi* is observed, which is garlanding with flowers. A return from a journey, recovery from an illness, the passing of an examination, or the achieving of any other success are all occasions for *gul-poshi*.

Custom and tradition decreed that one should look after the poor and needy of one's locality. The mosque of the *mohalla*, that is the vicinity where one lived, was a special care of the lady of the house.

In Ramadan, *iftari* is sent every evening and with great eclat on the seventeenth, twenty-first and twenty-seventh of the month. The expenses for *Khatm-i-Taraveeh,* and mosque repairs are undertaken as a matter of course. A lady of position knew that these things were expected of her and did them. She also knows what is not done, and what is done, and the manner in which to do it. And, though she did not sit on many committees for social welfare, she did not ignore the age-old customs by which the poor and the needy were looked after. This is more so in villages where families have been staying for generations.

Custom and tradition decree not only her action but even her manners. There were stringent rules as to whom she could talk to on familiar terms, and with whom her conduct should be one of gracious condescension. In the days when one's household consisted of more than a couple of hundred people, it was not an easy matter to know exactly what degree of familiarity or deference was expected from one by various members of the house, and yet a slight mistake in this would dub one an outsider.

Milady's
Household

III

ife behind the veil was certainly a world of its own. It had a complete hierarchy within its four walls, and in milady's household could be found a complete cross-section of society. A family in those days never consisted of only a married couple and their children. There were parents, grandparents, aunts and uncles, and cousins, to the second and third degree, so the members of a 'family' would, on the surface, be treated exactly alike. There was, however, a subtle difference between the actual masters and mistresses of the household and the various dependents and semi-dependent members of the family.

Then came the hierarchy of the servants. The highest, and perhaps the most influential of these, would be *Bi Mughlani*. Her specific duties are a bit difficult to describe; she combined in herself the role of a personal maid to the mistress, adviser-general and confidant, and it was in her capacity as the last two that she owed her importance, for the actual attendance on milady, and the stitching of her wardrobe were delegated to lesser beings. *Bi Mughlani* allocated to herself the task of administering general lectures on efficiency, loyalty, punctuality, etc., to the lower staff. She was always in attendance on Her Ladyship at home, and when she went visiting she sat next to her with the *pandan* before her, making *pans* or cutting *chhalia,* and keeping up a running commentary on life in general and on any subject that might be the topic of discussion for the time being.

It might be the latest affair of the household or the merits of purchasing a new pair of shoes. The ladies depended on her devotion and loyalty and, because of this, she succeeded in wielding a tremendous influence. Consequently, she was much sought after by those who would have a favour from Her Ladyship. No less a person than the lord and master of the house himself very often got the *Mughlani* to intercede for him!

Next to the *Mughlani* in influence and actual importance, but on the same social scale, perhaps somewhat higher, was *Ustaniji.* She was generally a pious lady who had performed at least one Hajj and had visited the Holy Places, and to whom was entrusted the education of the girls of the household. She took pride in the fact that she had taught successive generations of young ladies to read the Quran and to say their prayers. As *Bi Mughlani* was the source and fount of all gossip and was consulted on every social function, *Ustaniji* was the fount of all learning and wisdom and was referred to in the performance of religious ceremonies. She could always be relied upon to give her opinion with a great deal of dignity and reticence. Though all the ceremonies were performed year after year, yet, before undertaking anything, *Ustaniji's* advice was sought on each occasion as to whether it would be advisable to have such and such a ceremony on this or that date, and her verdict was final.

Very much lower on the social scale, yet an indispensable member of the household, was the *Nain*. She was the person responsible for all the comings and goings between the house and the outside world. She carried the good tidings of the birth of a child, and received the reward; she distributed invitations to weddings and was the source of news and gossip from the whole *mohalla*. At marriages, and various other ceremonies, she had a major role to play, and was a sort of general factotum for all the arrangements.

Anna was the wet nurse of the children, and a person of consequence in the household. In the house of the well-to-do, there would be a wet nurse per child and, as there were at least half a dozen children to each couple, there would be as many *Annas*. They would sometimes stay on and nurse other children of the family after having weaned the one for whom they were originally engaged, until they had nourished as many children as they possibly could. They had no specific duties assigned to them, but were generally held in a great deal of affection by the children they had suckled and, because of this, gained in importance when those children grew up and became masters and mistresses of their own households. They would then take on the job of supervising and bringing up those children, and be a most trusted and loyal servant of the household. Even those who went back to their homes after suckling only one child registered a permanent claim on the household for remuneration on all social occasions, such as *Eid* or *Baqr Eid,* and would come in for a great deal of attention on various occasions of the child's life, culminating in marriage.

On the last rung of the ladder were the *chhokris* or *laundies.* These were, strictly speaking, not slave girls in that they were not bought, and were free, theoretically, to go away whenever they wanted to, but for all practical purpose they were no better than slaves. Generally speaking, they were often those whose parents had been servants or attendants in the house. There was a constant recruitment of these *chhokris.* They were taken over from as early an age as four or five years and, in some cases, even a six-month old baby would be adopted into the household and one of the maid-servants given charge of her upbringing. There was, therefore, always a very large number of these girls in any household; each daughter of the house had one or two of these *chhokris* as her personal attendant. These girls did not have too bad a time. They were brought up to learn cooking, sewing, dyeing, laundering, etc. They managed to attain a great deal of polish and were, when older, often promoted to the status of *Mughlani* or *Anna.* They, together with the *Mamas* (equivalent to an English maid), did all the household chores such as sweeping and dusting, making of beds, cleaning of silver, washing of plates, etc. The more stupid ones spent their lives just charring, while the intelligent ones rose gradually to positions of importance, according to their special accomplishments or talents. They became expert cooks, or excelled in dyeing, so that all work of that kind was handed over to them, and thus, they avoided other menial tasks. Some learned to sing and dance, and joined the *mirasans* in entertaining their ladies on all festive occasions, or whenever they were in the mood for some light music and singing. *Mirasans* were the professional dancing girls, not of the highest grade but the kind that were engaged for minor festivities. They did not possess great musical knowledge, so as to be of use for *mujras* and dancing among men, but were good enough for brightening up various social occasions behind *purdah*. They lived outside the house generally, but each household had its own group of *mirasans*, and they came and went as regularly to the house, as did other servants. In a large household, or one of great opulence, there would be other sub-divisions of servants. There would, for example, be women in charge of stores known as *daroghas*. There would be a couple of junior *mughalanis* whose function would be only to stitch and sew. There would be a group of *laundies* trained only for entertainment, and they would have a fund of jokes, stories, rhymes and riddles at their disposal.

A household consisting of such heterogeneous elements was naturally far from harmonious. There would be jealousies and rivalries and intrigues and backbiting. But then that is life, and in the world behind the veil it was no less so. All its stresses and strains, all the highs and lows, and all the conflicts and tussles that go on in the world, found their reflection in life behind the veil. It was by no means silent, monotonous or dull. It was as throbbing with vitality and interest as the world outside. A staff as large as this is hardly possible now —

neither the size of the house nor the income permits it. Although the complete hierachy is no longer there, in many houses one still sees a few of these old retainers. They are a boon to their mistresses and the envy of all her friends. In villages, however, one still finds very large staffs in the houses of the landed gentry, for employment as domestic servants is the only means of earning a livelihood for the people of a country which is not yet fully industrialized.

The Pleasures of the Table

IV

hen civilization is at its height, food, clothing and all everyday activities take on the elaborateness of a work of art. So it happened when Moghul culture was at its height in the Indian subcontinent; food, dress, the way of life, social functions, all were surrounded with a hundred and one ceremonies.

Throughout the Middle East, the typical Muslim dish is *pulao* and *kebab,* which vary slightly in flavour, due to the adding or withholding of certain spices, but in the main are cooked in the same way and are the *piece de resistance* at any banquet. In Pakistan, these two characteristically Middle Eastern dishes are served with even more elaboration — saffron, almonds and raisins being added to them to give richness and to render them more delicious, though somewhat indigestible. Muslims have always been great meat-eaters, from the time when they roasted whole goats over their camp-fires in the deserts until now, and they eat meats of many kinds. The manner of eating has now changed, and now meat is served

in various ways, always very highly spiced. Grilling
and frying are the favourite methods of cooking;
boiling and steaming find no favour in the eastern
kitchen, but cooking *en casserole* is much in favour.
Pakistanis are bread eaters; they, however, do not
favour oven-baked bread. They eat unleavened
bread, but it is surprising how many varieties they
have achieved in this also. The most common form is
the *chapati* and the *abi-nan*. These can best be
described as unsweetened pancakes. Then we have
the *parathas;* these have *ghee* (clarified butter in
which all food is cooked) in its layers and look
something like puff-pastry. *Puri* is a small drum-like
bread fried in fat; but this is more popular in the
Hindu household than in the Muslim. At weddings,
banquets and feasts, *sheermals* and *baqar khanies* are
prepared; these are breads made of flour mixed with
milk and *ghee* and baked in an oven: they are
delicious but, like all our food, highly indigestible.
Food is served with great elaboration, and salty as
well as sweet dishes are decorated with great care.
Silver and gold wafers are put on all sweets, and fine
shreds of almonds and pistachio nuts are sprinkled
most tastefully on them, with currants dotted here
and there. *Pulao* rice is also invariably sprinkled with
saffron and almonds. Saffron is used in preparing
chicken as well as many other dishes that are
prepared *en casserole*. Rose-water is also lavishly
used in the preparation of sweets.

Fruits have always been very popular with the
Muslims and after their coming to India, the typical
Indian fruit, the mango, was cultivated by the
Muslims with great care. While originally only one
or two varieties were found, now, because of careful

grafting and cultivation, no less than a dozen varieties are produced. These cultivated varieties have a delicacy of flavour much excelling the ones that were originally found here. Mangoes grow at a time of the year when the rains begin, and mango parties are a favourite feature at this time of the year, each nobleman having beautiful mango gardens of his own. Another indigenous fruit that, by cultivation has reached great exquisiteness in taste and flavour, is the melon. While the ordinary variety of melon, as well as watermelon, is grown in every part of India and Pakistan, the river bed of the Gumti in Oudh was found particularly suitable for cultivating a very delicate variety. This particular type has an exquisite flavour, but its delicacy prevents it from its being transported any great distance.

Pan, a sort of green leaf which is eaten together with certain spices and tobacco, is also cultivated with great care, and there are more than a dozen varieties of it, each, for a *pan* eater, having a very distinctive taste; those used to a particular variety find the other variety quite unpalatable. There is the same snobbishness attached to the varieties of *pan* as there is to cigarettes. There is in it as great a range in quality as there is between *555* and *Scissors*. Most habitual *pan* eaters take tobacco with it, and here again there is the same variety and delicacy to be found. The tobacco used in *pan* is highly flavoured and makes the breath very sweet.

Chewing of various spices is also a favourite amongst Pakistanis and, here also, quality and flavour play a great part. Cardamom is the favourite spice and is served with or without *pan* on all social occasions. There are two or three varieties of this,

. and on social occasions, these are served wrapped in silver and gold wafers. Sometimes cardamom is boiled in milk and then dried and served; in this way the taste and flavour is improved. Spices are served singly or mixed together, and sometimes lightly coloured with saffron or mixed with shreds of almonds and currants, giving an added richness; these spices are served in silver boxes and very attractive silver boxes are made in beautiful designs for serving these spices. For everyday use, *batwas* are more popular. These are small pouches made of silk, satin, velvet or brocade and open and close by means of draw-strings.

Pakistan being a hot country, cold drinks have always been in great favour. Although tea is very popular now, in the really hot months it still gives way to *sherbet*, which is what the cold drinks are called by the Muslims. *Sherbets* are made in a dozen different varieties; the most popular is the ordinary sugar and water syrup, scented with rose-water or *keora*. Lemon juice squeezed in, makes it still more tasty. Milk *sherbets* are served on formal occasions and were popular here long before milk shakes became popular amongst us, milk *sherbet*, as well as all other kinds of *sherbets*, were always served with shreds of almonds and pistachio nuts in it.

All kinds of seasonal fruits find their way into *sherbets*. Different varieties of melon, as well as *jamuns*, *falsas*, and even mango juice, are squeezed and made into *sherbet*. The *sherbet* of the raw mango is supposed to ward off heat stroke, while the *sherbet* of a fruit called *bail* is specified for all stomach troubles. Like the English housewife who takes pride in making and bottling jams and jellies, in Pakistani households seasonal fruit is made into *sherbet* and kept in bottles to be served to visitors. Rose-water and *keora* are always added to enhance the taste. In summer, even ordinary drinking water has rose-water and *keora* mixed with it to make it more enjoyable, while water cooled in *surahis,* i.e., earthenware vessels, has a fragrance of its own. Certain foods are associated with certain festivals among the Muslims, as the Christmas cake is associated with Christmas, and Easter eggs with Easter. The Muslim festival of *Eid* is celebrated in the culinary line by the cooking of *siwaiyan.* These are somewhat like vermicelli, and are served in two or three ways — just boiled in milk and served with dried dates, or cooked in syrup and garnished with the usual gold and silver wafers, almonds, raisins and saffron. *Pulao,* of course, is always cooked on *Eid* days, but *siwaiyan* is the special dish for this occasion and is served to all visitors on that day, and a spoonful must be tasted by each. The Muslims also have an All Saints Day known as *Shab-i-Barat;* on this occasion, apart from prayers being offered and the poor being fed, a special kind of dish called *halwa* is prepared and served together with *chapatis, sheer mals* or *nans.* These are sent to friends' houses and distributed to the poor. Moharram, which is the Easter of the Muslims for it commemorates the martyrdom of the Prophet's grandson, Hazrat Imam Husain, is also observed with the cooking of special dishes. Various grains are mixed together with meat, and a most delicious sort of porridge is made of it. This is known as *haleem* or *khichra.* It is cooked on the ninth day of Moharram and the poor are fed on this day and given *sherbet* to drink lavishly in order

to give rest to the soul of Imam Husain who was denied water for three days. As this is a period of mourning, the *pan* eaters give up eating *pan* at this time, but various spices are mixed together with a great deal of taste and elaboration and served instead of *pan* and sent to the houses of friends as presents. These spices are known as *gota*, and are distributed in *batwas* made specially for the occasion.

Ramadan, the month of fasts, has its distinguishing dishes as well. These are known as *iftari*, and they are especially appetizing and light, something like hors-d'oeuvre, prepared to be eaten on breaking the fast, to be followed by a proper meal later on.

There are the lesser festivals with their characteristic dishes also; but these major ones would not be complete without these dishes, as one cannot imagine Christmas without turkey and Christmas cake. Shortage and scarcity in every sphere is forcing people to give up being particular about flavours and quality, and they are, therefore, thankful for what they can get; but on festive days, an all-out attempt is still made to keep up the traditions.

Varieties
in the
Wardrobe

V

hether behind the veil or outside it, women of Pakistan dress beautifully and colourfully, and in an amazing variety of styles. Saris are, of course, well-known in the West, and have been acclaimed as a most graceful and attractive dress. What is not realized in the West, however, is the numerous styles and fashions in which a sari can be worn. One would be inclined to think that the draping of six yards of material would not offer much scope for variety, but it is incredible what ingenuity the wearers of saris have shown in the making and wearing of them. The sari can be of plain white material with a coloured woven border; it can be plain or it can be printed. Saris can be obtained in georgettes, chiffons, silks and net, gold and silver tissues, with exquisitely woven borders, or borders that are stitched on; they can have tiny flowers all over or just one large sprig embroidered at an angle that falls just on the shoulders.

And fashions in saris are as varied as the style. 'How lucky you are. Your fashions never change,' sigh

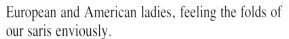

European and American ladies, feeling the folds of
our saris enviously.

'But they do!' we reply, though of course they do not
change as drastically and irrevocably as do the
fashions in dresses. They do change sufficiently and
definitely enough for a wearer to be considered a
person who dresses *a la mode* or an old-fashioned
one. Of course, the classic style of sari, i.e., one
with a woven border, and *palla* is never out of
fashion. But the ladies here seldom wear just that one
style of sari; more often they favour a plain georgette
or silk with a richly embroidered blouse, or one with
the narrowest of trimmings and a rich broad *palla*.
The sari most fashionable just now are the ones
known as the *patli-palla* saris. These have woven,
embroidered, or printed flowers only at the *palla*,
i.e., the portion that drapes off the shoulders, and at
the *patli*, i.e., the portion that falls in folds in front.
Sometimes a large spray embroidered in sequins will
be worn on the right shoulder of the blouse and the
same motif repeated at one angle of the *palla* or at
the waist. In short, the varieties in which saris are
worn would take pages to enumerate.

That is not all — Pakistani women do not wear just
one kind of dress in various styles but they wear
completely different styles of dresses as well. Each
province has its special dress; the Balochi, the
Kashmiris and the Sindhis, all wear dresses equally
rich in colour, but different in style, while the
Moghul Court dress, *gharara*, is in tremendous
vogue all over Pakistan. A *gharara* is a full divided
skirt cut in flares; with it is worn a *kurta*, that is a
tunic coming down to the knees, and a gossamer veil
on the shoulders. It is a very attractive and dressy

A bride in
farshi pyjama

Gharara
the Moghul court dress,
still worn on
formal occasions

dress. Women of taste wear it in a great variety of styles. *Kurta* and *dupatta*, i.e., the tunic and the veil, are sometimes worn to match; and sometimes one or both are in contrasting colours from the skirts. Great ingenuity and taste is displayed in the choice of colours, and a women's gathering where *gharara* is worn, looks like a veritable flower garden.

It is an expensive dress, reminiscent of the balmy days of the Muslims when they had made an art of the business of living, dressing and eating. Skirts are generally made of beautiful satin and brocade; the tunic is of a fine silk or, in summer, of gauze or net. This costume is a charming one and as graceful as a sari, but more elaborate, and lending itself to greater innovations of style. The skirt, tunic and veil are trimmed with lace or embroidered with gold thread. In the gold lace itself, which is called *gota*, there is an endless variety — each style of gold lace having a special name. The plain ribbon-like ones in silver or gold are known as *gota;* those that are embossed are called *thappas;* the crinkling ones are known as *gokhrus;* narrow braids are *bankris;* and gota twisted into little triangles is *champa*. Gold thread of an inch to three inches in width, worn at the edge of *dupattas*, make a really dazzling trimming. Gold laces are stitched round the veil, while the neckline and cuffs of the tunics are edged with it. The skirt, where it flares, has a narrow trimming of one of the various kinds of gold lace; or if it is for a really grand occasion, then the whole of the flared portion will be embroidered with gold thread or stitched with gold lace.

Stitching of gold lace is an art in itself and is done in a variety of ways. There are the traditional styles, of course, but ladies of fashion are forever inventing new modes, showing great ingenuity and originality in the use of these trimmings. Before a wedding or any great social function, the making and stitching of these dresses is carried on in great secrecy and, on the day of the actual function, great interest is shown in each other's dresses. Those who have achieved a really original effect are the object of envy for the less gifted ones.

This dress is one of a period of opulence and wealth. It seems perhaps out of place in the world of today, but it certainly gives a gala appearance to social functions, and makes us forget, at least for a short while, the grim reality which is all too present at every other time.

While the *gharara* is very kind to the figure, and even those who are not streamlined can wear it as it's graceful folds cover up many a defect, this cannot be said of the *churidar pyjama*, also known as the *tang pyjama*. These are close-fitting, breeches-like trousers, generally of exquisite satin of bright hues, with a kurta coming up to just below the knees, and a veil similar to that worn with a *gharara* thrown over the shoulders. This is a very attractrive dress also, but really becoming to those only who have a perfect figure. Young girls look very attractive in it and women who are not too tall do not look bad in them either, but this is certainly not the dress for those with plump figures. With *churidar pyjamas* is also worn the dress known as *peshwaz*. It can be described as a dress with a tight-fitting bodice and a very full skirt coming up to the knees. A *peshwaz* is always made of gold tissue or fine gauze, usually embroidered with gold thread or spangled with

The *tang pyjama*

Peshwaz

sequins. In old paintings the Moghul Empresses, Nur Jehan and Mumtaz Mahal, are seen wearing these. It is now hardly ever worn, even at marriages, though up till about forty years or so ago, it was the dress for all really formal occasions.

The most popular dress, however, and the one that has become the everyday dress of the women of Pakistan is the *shalwar,* with a tailored *kurta,* known as *kamiz,* and *dupatta.* This dress alone, of all the dresses worn amongst us, is the most practical and it has been modernized and stylized according to present day requirements. *Shalwars* are baggy trousers which narrow down at the ankles; the skirt worn with these trousers is now cut almost like a dress. The veil worn with *shalwars* is not of such gossamer texture as that worn with the *gharara* or the breeches-like trousers, but is of a thicker material and is worn as a scarf across the shoulders or draped over the shoulder. This dress has been adopted by professional women, for office work, sports, travel and everyday wear. I am sure this will remain the most popular dress in Pakistan, but there is a trait discernible in it which I find very alarming. This trait is the increasing westernization of the *kamiz,* i.e., the tunic worn with the *shalwars* and *ghararas;* they are now almost indistinguishable from the European dresses. They are cut on the same lines and given pleats and panels in the style of dresses, while the *dupatta* is getting shorter and shorter, both in length and breadth, and is thrown merely as a scarf round the shoulders. If it is done away with altogether, all that would then be required is the replacement of *shalwars* and *ghararas* by pants and we would have, almost imperceptibly, adopted the western dress.

This will be a pity, for we women of the Indo-Pakistan subcontinent, together with the women of the Far Eastern countries, are the only ones who have retained our own picturesque costumes. Sari, however, defies westernization, and I hope that the glamorous *ghararas* and the gorgeous *shalwars* and *kamiz* will not end in slick evening gowns and tailored evening dresses.

How Beauty Adorned Herself

VI

hile Western cosmetics are now the order of the day, and lipstick and nail polish have found their way into the smallest village store, the ways and means of enhancing beauty were not unknown earlier in the world behind the veil. Lips were reddened with *pan* and the use of *dandasa*, which is the bark of the walnut, while an added touch of sophistication was provided by *missi*, that is a specially prepared black powder, a thin line of which was drawn across *pan*-reddened lips. It looked most attractive, especially on fair women. Some rubbed *missi* on the teeth also, it gave a blackish hue to them, and blackened edges were supposed to be as attractive as black pearls. We, who are now used to admiring pearl-white teeth, might not agree that this is so, but fashion is a matter of taste and of getting used to an idea. I have seen women with *missi*, and it does give an air of sophistication which no western cosmetic can vouchsafe. Use of *missi* was strictly forbidden for unmarried girls, although an occasional *pan* was permissible.

Long before nail polish became the vogue in Europe, *mehndi* was used not only to redden the nails but the entire plam of the hand and the sole of the feet. But applying of *mehndi* was by no means an easy task. It did not mean the mere smearing of the paste on the whole palm — it was applied, by means of a fine hair brush, in various designs, the more popular being the crescent and star, a heart, or some floral decoration. Sometimes just one large dot was placed on to the middle of the palm; sometimes small dots were placed all over it. Only on the wedding day was *mehndi* applied to the entire palm. A thin red line of *mehndi* stretched over the knuckles looked very becoming on fair hands. Light tints were not liked; the brighter the hue, the better it was liked. *Mehndi* grown in certain areas is supposed to give a redder hue than others, and *mehndi* picked during the time of *barsat* was supposed to be of the brightest hue; therefore, the applying of *mehndi* was most popular at this time of the year. Girls kept dried leaves of *barsat mehndi* for applying at other times of the year, when such good quality leaves were not available. Dark eyes were darkened further by the application of *surma* and *kajal*. *Surma* is powdered antimony, and *kajal* is lamp-soot, which is prepared by burning specially perfumed oils and covering the flame with an earthern cup and scraping up the moist soot in little silver boxes. *Kajal* glistens, while *surma* does not, and is more alluring; consequently, *kajal* is preferred by the younger ones, and *surma* by the more sedate.

Nor was skin care unknown in those days. As a matter of fact, judging from the excellent condition

Above:
Applying henna

Left:
Flowers formed
an indispensable
part of a
lady's toilet

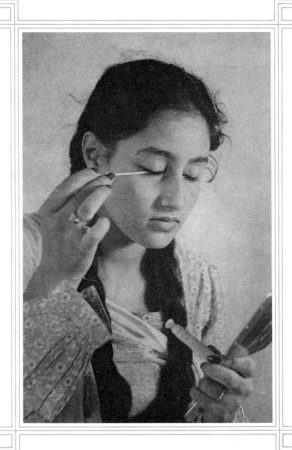

A silver slide
is used to put
surma in the eyes

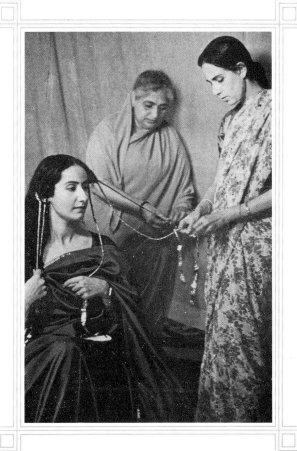

Braiding the hair
with gold tinsel

of older women's complexions, their's was a better way. Use of soap for the face was not favoured; the face was washed with *ubatna*, that is a powder especially prepared from sweet-smelling herbs which have a beneficial effect on the skin; this was rubbed all over the body also, and was removed with oil. The preparation of *ubatna* took a lot of time and has, therefore, been given up in these days of hurry but it is still prepared at the time of weddings. Orange peel was dried and powdered and used for softening the skin; almonds ground in milk were supposed to soften the skin; and were used during the winter, while lemon juice with *sohaga*, i.e., borax, was used during the summer and was supposed to guard against pimples. Sea shells soaked in milk was another remedy for skin blemishes, while washing the face with the milk of green coconuts was a sure cure for pimples and other adolescent disfigurements. In fact, the ladies behind the veil knew much more about keeping the complexion young and beautiful. They did not use things out of jars that merely hide blemishes, but they knew the ways and means of avoiding the blemishes.

Perfumes were lavishly used in milady's toilet. A silver box containing six or eight of her favourite scents always stood at her dressing table, and she used them according to her mood, the occasion, and the season of the year. Cool *khas* for the hot summer days, *gulab*, *motia* and *chambeli* for *sawan*, and rich heavy *suhag* for winters and for weddings.

From the day of her wedding, flowers formed an indispensable part of a lady's toilet. The bridal bed was covered by a lacelike tracery of flowers; the bride and groom wore, and still wear *sehras* on the wedding day; and on the fourth day all the bride's jewellery is made of flowers alone. Every day flowers are worn by ladies around the neck, on the wrists, and twined around the hair. Gold circlets are threaded with flowers, and these are worn like earrings. The use of flowers or dabbing even a drop of *itr* is forbidden to young and unmarried girls. While talking about *itr,* one is reminded that the *Itr of Roses* was discovered by the Empress Nur Jehan. It is said that the Queen always had roses floating in her bath water and that, one day, she noticed a speck of oil on the water and immediately realized that it was the extract of the rose.

A most exotic touch was given to make-up by the use of *afshan* and *chamki,* that is a fine gold dust sprinkled upon the hair and face, and gold sequins cleverly gummed and stuck on the hair. This is no longer in vogue, and only on a wedding day and for a few months immediately after the wedding do young girls decorate themselves in this glamorous fashion today. In the past, they went on using this glamorous addition to their make-up for several years after the wedding. But, here again, there was an unwritten law which decided the age and time after which such adornment should be given up, while one could and did use flowers right up to old age. *Afshan* and *chamki* were only for the very young and the newly-wed; those who continued to use it later on, after the first bloom of youth, were subjected to ridicule. Also there was, and even today there is, some mysterious law known to ladies only which decrees at which juncture make-up exceeds the boundary of seemliness; and, like all the world over, one of the things that denotes a lady is the restraint and good taste shown in her make-up.

Jewels of
the Past

VII

he Orient has always been famous for its jewellery. In the Indian subcontinent, during the Moghul period, jewellery of great beauty and exquisite craftsmanship was made. Despite the wars, revolutions, and mutinies, that have ravaged this part of the world, many of the exquisite old objects of this period are still to be found, for pieces have been handed down from mother to daughter for generations. The Moghul period was really wonderful in its skill in every branch of the arts and crafts. In jewellery, in particular, it excelled itself. Never has the human mind produced so many varieties of jewellery as was produced during this period. Each article of jewellery — earring, necklace, bracelet, armlet, pendant — was made in a number of styles, each having a separate name and known not only as a necklace or a bracelet but by the name that described its origin as well. Some of the names have most interesting histories behind them, and most of them are extremely poetic. There is a necklace known as *champa kali*, meaning 'buds of *champa'* (frangipani), another as *chandan-har,* meaning 'the firefly'. Necklaces worn close to the throat are called *gulu-band,* while strings of beads are called *seh-laras, puch-laras,* or *sath-laras,* according to the number of strings in them; bracelets are known as *phonchi, kangan, kara, chuhi-danti, Jahangiri,* and so forth. The *Jahangiri* was designed by the Empress Nur Jehan to cover a scar on her wrist.

The story of how she came by the scar is an interesting one, and goes like this. The Queen, Nur Jahan, was practising archery inside the Agra Fort, when an arrow went astray; it flew over the ramparts to the other side of the river where some washermen were washing clothes. The arrow struck one of the washermen, and he died. His poor wife distraught with grief pulled the chain of the Bell of Justice that hung above the doors of the Fort. Emperor Jahangir appeared almost immediately on the balcony and said, as was his wont, 'Here I am plantiff. Tell me what ails you?'

The woman told her story and the Emperor listened to it with attention and then asked her to appear before the court the next day. He promised her justice would be done. The Emperor then withdrew and made enquiries as to who was practising archery at that time. It transpired that the Queen was. Jahangir heard the report gravely. After pondering over the matter for sometime, he gave orders that the Queen be bereft of all royal trappings and be taken to the prision cells under the Fort with orders to appear before the court and the *dhoban* (washerwoman) the next morning.

The order was carried out. The next morning as the

Emperor sat on his golden throne, the *dhoban* appeared. The Emperor asked her to repeat her story. She did. Then the King ordered that Nur Jahan be brought in to hear the charge against her. After this was done, Jahangir turned to the *dhoban* and picking up the bow and arrow that lay at the foot of the throne said, 'This women has widowed you. Islamic Justice entitles you to exact revenge. Take this bow and arrow and widow her by shooting me.'

The poor woman was horrified. There was pandominium in the court. All began entreating the *dhoban* to accept compensation in lieu of life, which is acceptable in Islam. The poor woman falteringly agreed.

Before the sum could be fixed, the nobles and grandees of the court, began showering jewels, ropes of pearls, and golden sovereigns on the woman. Soon a king's ransom was collected and the woman went away bemused and grateful.

The queen was taken back to the Palace. No word of reproach had passed her lips for she knew a Muslim King has to do justice.

But Islamic law, like Biblical law says, 'an eye for an eye, a tooth for a tooth'. So, 'blood for blood,' said the *ulema*. 'The Queen's blood must be shed in expiation as *khoon baha*, (خوں بہا)

So, a small incision was made on the Queen's delicate wrist, and blood was allowed to flow in deference to the letter of the law. The incision left a scar. To hide the scar the Queen, forever innovative, designed a broad, studded braclet. This came to be known as the *Jehangiri*.

It is also called *phonchi* that is 'wristlet', and at times *chuhi danti*, as the studs look like the fine teeth of a mice.

All this jewellery was made in traditional styles and the craftsmanship passed down from father to son. There is a great variety in the traditional styles, and the method of setting stones, cutting, enamelling and matching them is one which has been practised for generations. A great feature of this splendid Moghul oriental jewellery is that much of it is worn threaded and not set in gold like most Western jewellery. The threading itself is a work of art and is done in many ways. It gives greater variety to the jewellery, and as the threading is more adjustable than gold, a better fit is achieved. Precious stones are set on gold and exquisite enamelling is done on the reverse side to the one on which the stones are set. So exquisite is the enamelling that this is as beautiful and, in some cases, more beautiful than the upper side. All really good pieces of ancient jewellery were made in this way; the less expensive pieces do not have enamelling on the reverse side. Stones were not highly polished or very regularly cut in these old pieces; their charm lies in their mellow colouring and irregularity. Not much old jewellery in gold can be found today because gold readily lent itself to being broken up and made into newer styles with very little loss of actual value. But even gold jewellery of about a hundred years ago is of a craftsmanship which cannot be matched today, and one wonders what the heights of perfection were which must have been achieved in the Moghul times in this branch of craftsmanship.

Hair Ornaments

Teeka — This is a pendant suspended on a string of pearls and worn on the forehead exactly at the angle at which the hair is parted. Nearly every bride wears this on her wedding day, and newly-weds continue to wear it for some years on every gala occasion. With this is worn, at a very cute angle on one side of the head, a piece of jewellery known as the *jhoomar*. This is a lacelike affair of pearls and diamonds. Instead of these two separate pieces, some women prefer wearing a *sarasari*. This is a jewelled pendant in the centre, with a gold chain studded with jewels tied on either side of the head. This looks something like a tiara.

Earrings

Earrings are worn in various styles and have very picturesque names:

- There is the *karan phul,* meaning 'radiant flower'. This corresponds to the Western 'ear tops', and is available in many styles but the traditional one is a flower-like affair with petals shaped like the rays of the sun. *Karan-phul* is worn by itself or with *jhumkas* attached to it. These are suspended from the *karan-phul* and look like little bells edged with pearls. A pearl circlet with a pin to attach it to the hair gives additional support and adds to the attractiveness of the earring.
- *Chand-bali* and *bijlian* are rather similar in style. *Chand-bali* means 'Moon hoop', and is made like a hoop with a small pendant inside

Sarasari

The reverse and
obverse sides of a
pair of earrings
with the fish
as its main motif

and another suspended from it. *Bijlian,* which means 'lightning', is a jewelled semi-circle with a pendant suspended from its outer edge. These pendants are always shaped to look like fish. So are the earrings known as *machhlian;* these are worn on a plain gold circlet. Fish was the court emblem of the kings of Oudh, like the French fleur-de-lis — hence their adoption in the designs of jewellery. The delicacy and beauty of these motifs defies descriptions; they were things of most exquisite workmanship.

- *Balians* were large plain gold circles with a few tiny flowers carved on one side of them. *Pattas,* which means 'leaves', because they were leaf shaped, were worn suspended through the *balians* when worn for gala occasions. Nowadays, *pattas* are worn just as plain earrings or a very pretty necklace is made from a set of them. In fact, most of the jewellery formerly worn around the arms or anklets have now been turned into necklaces or bracelets, as the fashion of wearing armlets and anklets, has gone out.

Necklaces

Necklaces are made in as varied styles as earrings. The classic piece of jewellery worn around the neck is the *gulu-band,* which means 'neck collar' and looks exactly what its name suggests — a collar of pearls or of gold, studded with jewels. Below the *gulu-band* were worn three or five or seven strings of pearls, known as *seh lari, puch lari* or *sat lari.* Each of the strings had a small pendant hanging from it.

A *guluband*
showing the
enamelling on the
reverse side

A most attractive necklace is one known as *champa-kali*, which means 'buds of champa' (champa is a magnolia-like flower with an exquisite scent). *Hansli, dugduqi, thussi* and *chandan-har* are some of the many styles of necklaces that were popularly worn.

Armlets

Nauratan, joshan, and *bazuband* are all armlets of different styles:

- *Nauratan* means 'nine jewels', for it consists of nine small tablets, each studded with a different precious stone and strung together; nowadays it makes a most attractive set of necklace and bracelet.
- *Joshan* had small cylinders of gold, studded with jewels and strung together like the *nauratan* and, like it, now makes a very attractive necklace and bracelet set.
- *Bazuband* was a broad piece of gold and enamel jewellery worn on the arm, and it now makes a very effective bracelet.

Bracelets

Apart from these other pieces of jewellery that have now been made into bracelets, there is a great variety in the styles of traditional bracelets themselves. The most popular jewellery worn around the wrist are the *chooris*, that is to say four to six very thin gold, pearl, or jewel-studded bracelets worn together. Then there are the slightly broader ones known as *patris* which are worn with an equal number of *chooris* on either side, or by themselves. In front of the *chooris* were worn *karas*, which are cylindrical shaped bracelets with bud-like endings. *Kangans* are yet another style of bracelet and they have little spikes all around them. *Jahangiri* is the bracelet which the Empress Nur Jehan invented to hide her scar, and it is as popular even today as it was in the days of that great queen.

Rings

These are very popular and are worn a good deal. There is a very attractive style of bracelet known as *dast-phul*, which combines the bracelet and ring into one piece of jewellery; there was another very attractive style in rings known as *arsi*. This was a little mirror set amidst stones.

Anklets

Except for village women or brides, no one wears jewellery around the ankles these days (although the fashion does seem to be coming back now), but these pieces of jewellery were of exquisite workmanship and have been turned into most gorgeous looking necklaces. There were many varieties in anklets also, as in other pieces of jewellery. There were the *karas* and *chharas*, which could be described as the opposite number to *karas* and *chooris* worn around the wrist. There were the *lachhas*, that is, twenty or more very fine gold circlets worn all together. Then there was the most attractive of ankle jewellery known as *pazaib*, which had bells that tinkled in a fascinating manner when the wearer moved.

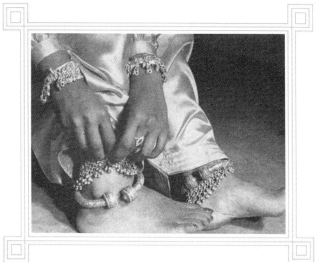

Pazeb

Jewellery box

Ghungrus which, gave out a regular peal were worn only by little girls or by dancing girls, so ladies did not wear them.

The sophisticated ladies at the court and palace never wore jewellery around the waist. These were only worn by village women, as were the large nose rings. For milady, a single priceless diamond or ruby, whose value would be above pearls, sufficed for the nose ring, but tradition decreed that on the wedding day, just for a few hours, she wore the *nath*, that is the large nose ring. But now that is completely out of fashion, for girls do not pierce their noses any more. But the *nath* is still handed down from mother-in-law to daughter-in-law as an heirloom.

Wedding

VIII

Muslim marriage in Pakistan is indeed a ceremonious thing. It used to take days — sometimes weeks — to celebrate a really grand orthodox Muslim wedding, for there are innumerable customs and rituals to be performed in connection with a marriage, each of them extremely pretty and having some significance. Even now, when the ceremonies have been cut down to the minimum, it takes at least a week to celebrate a wedding, though, of course, some very modern people have just the plain religious ceremony followed by a reception. In such a wedding the only eastern element is the gorgeous dress of the bride, but such marriages are like the registry office marriages of the West and are still an exception. Most families like making the marriage of their son or daughter as colourful as they can.

The all-absorbing occupation of making of dresses by the ladies of both sides of the family starts months ahead, for the bride receives not only a trousseau from her mother but numerous sets of dresses from

her would-be in-laws, as well. The wedding dress also is provided by the bridegroom's family, therefore, great preparations go on, on both sides. The groom's dress is provided by the bride's people, and is perhaps the only occasion in which nowadays in the East, a man's dress is truly in the gorgeous eastern style. The traditional bridal colour is red, and the bride's dress is always a bright vermillion or shocking pink. The *gharara*, or the skirt, is of rich gold brocade; the tunic is of crepe, *banarsi* or silk; and the veil is of the finest silk available, heavily embroidered with gold or stitched with rows upon rows of various kinds of gold lace.

A bridal veil is truly a cloth of gold, dazzling the eyes and taking one's breath away. The bridegroom's dress is a *sherwani*, that is, a long buttoned coat coming down to the knees. It is generally of gold brocade with which are worn close-fitting breeches like trousers of beautiful thick white or cream silk or satin, and a *banarsi* turban is tied on the head, while gold-embroidered shoes on the feet complete the outfit. Both the bride and the bridegroom wear on their forehead a lacelike affair of flowers and gold thread, known as *sehra*. This has the same significance as orange blossoms in the West, that is to say, only those getting married for the first time can wear it. Besides the bride and groom, several members on either side of the family come in for new sets of clothes as well. The bridegroom provides dresses for the bride's sisters and cousins; the bride's mother, on the other hand, gives dresses to the bridegroom's mother, sisters and to other close relatives. Old friends of the family, as well as family servants, are all given new clothes as presents on the

Ladies from the
bride's side
waiting to welcome the
bridegroom's family
for the *mehndi*

Above:
Guests, Princess
Basma (R) and
Princess Muna (L)
waiting for the
bride to appear
for the *mehndi*
ceremony

Left:
The bride
comes in escorted
by two of
her friends

Friend puts
henna
on the palm of
the bride

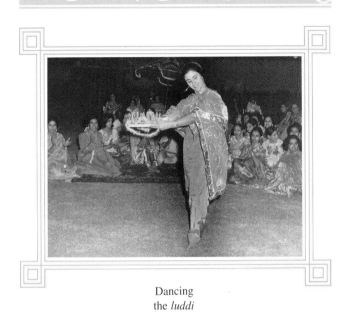

Dancing
the *luddi*

occasion of a marriage. Therefore, buying, sewing and stitching for months ahead is the all-occupying activity of a household where a marriage is pending. Each set of a bride's dress has shoes, bags, bangles, and other accessories to match.

The ceremonies begin three days before the actual wedding takes place. The first of these is known as the *Lagan* or *Manjha* ceremony. The bridegroom's mother takes a set of yellow or saffron coloured robes for the bride, together with perfumes, scented oil and *ubatna* (this is a preparation made of all sorts of scented herbs, and is very good for the complexion). Scents, oils and *ubatna* are all taken in beautifully made silver boxes and cut-glass bottles. Everything is arranged tastefully on silver trays and covered with tray-cloths embroidered with gold thread and edged with gold lace. Servants carry these trays on their heads from the bridegroom's house to the bride's and make a very picturesque procession. The most attractive tray is of *mehndi;* this is a leaf paste which is used for colouring the nails in lieu of the western nail polish. *Mehndi* is put on a silver tray, and a dozen or more small candles are lighted around it, and thus carried from the bridegroom's house to the bride's. Sometimes the procession is accompanied by instrumental bands as well. After the arrival of the procession, the ladies of the bridegroom's family arrive; they are greeted with garlands of flowers and drinks of *sherbet* at the bride's house; then the bride is brought out and seated in the centre of a large room; the bridegroom's mother and sisters touch the bride's forehead with *ubatna* then they put *mehndi* on her fingers, after which she is taken back to her room and a general sprinkling of *ubatna* over each other begins. This is a very gay occasion, and the young particularly enjoy this to their heart's content, soaking each other thoroughly with water in which *ubatna* and *mehndi* are mixed. This ceremony sets the tone for the merriment and festivites of the days that follow.

The next day, a similar procession leaves the bride's house for the bridegroom's. This is known as the *Mehndi*, as the putting of *mehndi* by the bride's sister on the bridegroom's finger is the reason for this ceremony. On this occasion, the bridegroom receives a set of clothes suitable for informal wear and all toilet accessories, such as soap, brush, comb, shaving set, mirror, etc. These are generally of silver, beautifully embossed and enamelled. These presents are brought by the younger sisters or sisters-in-law of the bride, and this is an occasion for a great deal of fun and frolic and backchat between them and the bridegroom.

The young visitors are received with much ceremony and eclat. After they have been seated and served with *pan* and *sherbet*, the bridegroom is sent for. He comes dressed in the suit of clothes just brought for him by the young ladies, and sits on a small silver or enamelled stool which has also come as a present from the bride's side. In rich households, the stool was made of pure silver; otherwise, it is of wood, painted or lacquered red. For an hour or so, a volley of badinage is exchanged between the bridegroom and the bride's sisters or cousins. Then the youngest of the bride's sisters or cousins gets up and, taking a little *mehndi*, puts it on the tip of the bridegroom's little finger. After having done that, she refuses to let go his hand unless he pays her ransom; brisk

The bride's sister
puts a dab of henna
on the groom's hand

Left:
The bridegroom,
Prince Hassan, and
his brother,
King Hussain of
Jordan, sitting
under a canopy
of flowers

Below:
President Ayub
Khan and
King Hussain
witness the
signing of the
nikah-nama

bargaining goes on, the bridegroom trying to get off as cheaply as possible, and the girls trying to get as big a sum as possible. The elders look on with tolerant amusement until they feel that a reasonable sum has been offered — then they intervene and entreat the girl to release her victim, which she does with great reluctance. All this fun helps to break the ice between the families of the groom and the bride. After the bride's sister has exacted her due, the bridegroom's sisters turn comes, who, after having touched his forehead with a bit of sandalwood paste, demand their presents; they, together with the girls who have come from the bride's side, receive, like the bridesmaids in the European wedding, similar presents. The bridesmaid-in-chief, however, receives a complete set of clothes, together with whatever else the others receive, plus her *naig*, which is the ransom money. But this is just the beginning. There will be several other occasions on which she will claim, and get, compensation! In fact, an elder brother's or sister's wedding is an event which helps the young people's financial position considerably more than *Eid* or *Baqr Eid*.

The *mehndi* procession returns late at night to the bride's house. The next day is the great day of the wedding. On this day, a few hours before the actual time of the wedding, *sachaq* arrives at the bride's house. This is yet another procession, bringing the rest of the gifts from the bridegroom's house. It has the bride's dress on a large silver tray, together with scents, oils, silver brush and comb, scents in silver bottles, gold embroidered shoes, and besides the wedding dresses, seven, eleven or twenty-one dresses, the number depending on what one can afford. Among the presents for the bride, there are dozens and dozens of jars of dried fruits and dozens of trays of sweetmeats to be distributed among friends. Also, there are tied in silk handkerchiefs or in coloured bags a few almonds, a few bits of sweets, and a few dates. These are distributed immediately after the wedding ceremony among all the guests present. In former days, all this was carried by servants from one house to the other, but now unless the distance is not much, these are taken in cars to the accompaniment of music and lighted torches. There is great excitement in the bride's house on the arrival of *bari*. All the presents are critically surveyed and appraised, and blame apportioned according to whether they come up to expectation or not. The bridal dress is carried into the bride's room together with a casket known as the *sohagpura*, which is made either of gaily coloured paper or red satin embroidered with gold. Inside this bag are various scented herbs which were formerly used by ladies for scenting or washing their hair, and for putting in their clothes as sachets. In this packet is put a present for the bride's sister or the bride's best friend, whose duty it is to open the *sohagpura*. Before the excitment of the *bari* dies down, the bridegroom's procession is heralded in. Formerly, the bridegroom rode on a horse saddled and bridled in gold cloth and gold chains in right royal style, but now most bridegrooms fight shy of this and prefer arriving in a saloon car bedecked with flowers. Next to the bridegroom in the car sits his brother or one of his best friends, besides one or two young boys of the family known as *shah bala*. His car is followed by friends and relatives and their cars; the procession

The bride and groom with
sehras on. A *sehra* is a veil
woven with golden threads and
pearls (seed pearls in this case) worn
till the *arsi mushaf*, that is till
before the groom sees the
bride's face

Above:
arsi mushaf –
one of the
prettiest
ceremonies
of the wedding

Left:
Princess Sarvath
after the
arsi mushaf

Bride with bridegroom,
sisters and cousin
after the
arsi mushaf
(Begum Ikramullah
is seated to the
right of the
bridegroom)

is acompanied with lights and a band, if it is an orthodox wedding. In a modern wedding, a band in the bride's house takes the place of a band accompanying the procession. The bride's house is always lighted with innumerable fairy lights; the gateway is decorated with lights and arches of flowers; fireworks are set off as the procession draws near. In fact, everything is calculated to make the atmosphere as festive and the scene as decorative as possible. The actual Muslim marriage ceremony is a very simple affair and takes place within five minutes; it is a plain and simple contract drawn up between the man and woman, the woman being represented by proxy as it is not customary for her to appear in public. The person who acts as her proxy is generally, a close member of her family; he goes into the *zenana*, together with two other male members of the family, and asks the girl to authorize him to act on her behalf. This she does within the hearing of the two witnesses after which the three come out to where the guests are gathered and the marriage ceremony takes place. The special feature of the Muslim marriage is the settlement of *mehr*, that is a sum of money to be paid by the bridegroom to the bride; without this settlement a marriage is not considered legal.

After the actual wedding ceremony, i.e., *nikah*, is over, many more formalities have to be gone through before the bride leaves for her new home. A grand feast follows the *nikah*, and most of the male guests depart after this. From now on, the ceremonies are exclusively confined to the female members of the families.

The bridegroom's meeting the bride and getting a

first glimpse of her face, is a most charming ceremony, known as *arsi-mushaf*. This takes place late in the evening, a good few hours after the *barat*, that is to say the arrival of the bridegroom's procession at the bride's house. All of this time is taken up in dressing the bride, and at the end of it she really looks like a fairy queen. Fingers and toe-nails are reddened with *mehndi*, fragrant herbs having been rubbed on her body for several days previously. This is followed by a scented bath, after which she puts on the wedding dress — always a gorgeous affair in red and gold. The hair is done in a most elaborate style; gold-sequins and gold dust called *afshan* are sprinkled on the hair to look like stars on an inky sky. Lips are reddened with *pan*, and a light dusting of *afshan* on the face adds a further glamorous touch. This is the day of days for jewellery; on her hair, around her neck on her wrists and arms, and on her feet, she wears jewellery of exquisite workmanship. After her toilet is complete, a *sehra* of gold lace and flowers is put on her forehead.

Dressed and bedecked like this, she is taken to the drawing-room by her friends and seated on the *masnad*, that is, an embroidered velvet carpet in the centre of the room. The bridegroom is now sent for, but before he can gain entrance, the bride's younger sister barricades his way and, unless tipped generously, will not let the bridegroom proceed. From the entrance of the drawing-room he is escorted by his sisters, to the place where the bride is sitting. The sisters throw a part of their *dupatta* over his head and bring him along under its cover. Thus he arrives at the *masnad*, and is made to sit facing the bride; a beautiful mirror is put between them, and a gossamer veil is thrown over both. A copy of the Quran is handed over to the bridegroom and he is asked to read a certain verse from it; after he has done that, he is asked to look into the mirror and see in it the reflected image of his bride. Many songs are sung while this ceremony is in progress, and much laughing and teasing goes on between the bridegroom and the bride's sisters and cousins. After the bridegroom has seen the bride's face, he puts a ring on the first finger of her right hand and touches her forehead with sandalwood paste, then he takes some of the sweet served in a silver tray and puts it on the bride's lips — the significance of all this being that may their life together always be fragrant and sweet. Now the most touching moment of the marriage draws near. The bride's father is sent for to hand over his daughter to the bridegroom. Most wistful songs, portraying the feeling of the bride, are sung at this moment, and as the bride takes her leave all dissolve in tears. At last the bride takes her leave and departs for her new home.

On arriving there, her entrance is stopped by the bridegroom's sister, and once again the poor bridegroom has to cough up some money before he and his bride are let in. After they have been seated, the bridegroom's sisters come with a silver bowl and wash the bride's feet and sprinkle the water on all corners of the house. The ceremony is meant to welcome the bride to her new house, and to signify a long life. The day after the wedding there is a feast at the bridegroom's house known as the *valima*. The bride's brothers come over after the *Valima*, to take the bride home, bringing with them quantities of sweets to be distributed among the bridegroom's family. On her return to her parents' house another ceremony known as *chouthi*, is performed. This is a most hilarious ceremony and marks the end of the wedding week. It is a sort of game played by pelting flowers and fruits, all of which are supplied by the bridegroom's people. It begins with a mock contest between the bride and the bridegroom, in which the bride invariably wins, after which the guests indulge in an all-out pelting of each other. This is a sort of grand finale to the wedding ceremony. All told, a wedding takes about eight days. One heaves a sigh of relief when it is all over for, though full of fun, they are certainly the most exhausting days imaginable. There is certainly more than an element of theatre in an orthodox eastern wedding. The entire ceremony is like a tableau in which each person performs a certain part in a certain manner.

A hundred and one ceremonies have been thought out only to add gaiety to the occasion. Not only marriages, but every other occasion, such as the birth of a child, birthdays, etc., were seized upon as an occasion for celebration and merrymaking, for life was leisured and money was plentiful in those days.

The photographs for this chapter have been taken from the wedding photographs of Begum Ikramullah's youngest daughter, Sarvath, to the Crown Prince of Jordan, Hassan.

The Gentle Art of Flirtation

IX

ur society was too sophisticated not to provide opportunities for the gentle art of flirtation, which added spice and gaiety to life even behind the veil.

'Really Sughra! You do exaggerate in your efforts to prove that life in *purdah*, or as you call it in your book, *behind the veil*, was not dull or drab but full or colour and fun. We do admit that you have painted a very attractive picture of it, but honestly how could there be any flirtation when women were in such strict *purdah* that, as you yourself say, nobody could even get a glimpse of them?' چشمِ فلک ــ نے نہ دیکھا جن کے دامن کو

'That was so', I would reply, 'But as I am trying to tell you, our society was too sophisticated a society not to allow for harmless dalliance between the sexes. This was done by making flirtations almost obligatory between certain relationships, such as between brothers and sisters-in-law of both sides. The sisters of the wife, the *salis*, as they were called, in particular always teased their brothers-in-law, and kept up an unending banter with him. He replied in kind.

The girls if they were young enough appeared before their brothers-in-law, and talked to him face to face. If they were teenagers, however, they did not appear before their brothers-in-law, but this did not cramp their style in any way, they continued making an endless series of provocative remarks from behind the *purdah,* playing practical jokes, and generally making his life a misery, or lively, depending on how you look at it.

The same happened between the husband's younger brothers and their brother's wife *(bhabi). Purdah* was not observed between them and the *bhabi* was the butt of the *dewar's* teasing and double-edged compliments. I had two younger brothers-in-law, both much older than me but both called me *Bhabi* and treated me with respect, but with tongue-in-check.

The older of my two brothers-in-law, Ahmad, I always said, was like a typical *dewar* in an Urdu novel. He remembered endless *ashaars* (couplets) which he quoted adlib very aptly, on every occasion. Brides, at the time I got married, remained veiled for quite some time after their marriage, especially before visitors. Ahmad would come and see me sitting demurely on the *takht* in the sitting-room or out in the *dalan* for it was summer time, and would hum an appropriate verse or two. I still remember some of it.

اللہ کسی صورت ٹوٹے تو حجاب اُن کا
اسے بادِ صبا تو ہی اُلٹ ا دے نقاب اُن کا

Later, when I had gotten over my initial shyness and

had begun going about the house more or less in a
normal manner, Ahmed once came upon me soon
after I had washed my hair, and with a twinkle in his
eyes commented that I really did have very long and
thick hair.

گُندھا نظر گزر کا پہننا نے گی آپ کو

ناپتی ہے زلفِ رسا سر سے پیر تک

On another occasion we were both sitting on either
side of my mother-in-law, who had been ailing for
some time. She asked for something. Both Ahmad
and I got up simultaneously to get it and give it to
her, and in doing so we came fairly close. Ahmad
sniffed, 'Ah! *Evening in Paris*,' he said. 'But how
do you know,' said I in my naive manner for I was
very young and guileless. 'Ah'! said Ahmad with a
wicked smile. He then recieted the following verse,

عُمر گزری ہے اِسی دشت کی سیاحی میں

and so it went on. I will not mutilate these
verses by translating them, but leave for those who
know Urdu to enjoy them.

Even my younger brother-in-law who eventually
became Chief Justice and Vice-President of India,
and was of a much more serious disposition from the
beginning, was not above some gentle teasing.
'Would you reveal your face to the vulgar gaze once
more,' he would say when yet another visitor was
shown in to see the new bride. It was difficult to
suppress a giggle at such an introduction to the
unveiling, but I tried to keep a straight face.
He was the one who found the 'courage', as he used
to say, to detach me from my weeping relatives and
bring me down to the car, otherwise we would have
missed the train he would say in a tone that seemed

to imply that he had performed an act of great valour.

Brides in my time were not any thing radiant, like the *Radiant Bride*. Leaving their father's house they wept copiously, and so did their relatives and even the men were not above becoming sentimental and surreptiously wiping tears from their eyes when saying goodbye to their little girls.

The father at such a moment was the one most deeply moved, and there are any number of songs from time immemorial, describing the emotions of farewell between the father and daughter. My father and I were more than usually attached to each other, and I was practically hysterical with tears as I clung to my father. It was at this stage that, as Hadi used to say, he had the 'unpleasant duty of wrenching me away'.

A similar scene was repeated at the time of the wedding of his nephew and again, as Hadi said, it fell to his lot to prise the weeping bride away from her brothers.

'I don't know why the unpleasant task of taking the girl away from her family always falls to my lot,' Hadi grumbled, 'I have not yet taken any one's daughter away!' for though the uncle of the bridegroom he was still, at that time, unmarried.

I mention these annecdotes to give an idea of the sort of banter that used to take place. As I write this, I remember any number of innocently teasing remarks and retorts between *dullah bhais* and *salis* and *dewars,* and *bhabis*. It was all very harmless, but made for a little bit of fun.

Flirtation is not a modern innovation. It has existed from time immemorial. It was a part of the pattern of our society. My mother used to relate amusing anncedotes of her brothers-in-law, particularly my father's witty remarks to his *bhabi* when she was a new bride.

So, as I said to my friends, 'Have I proven my point?' In fact there was nothing that was not fun, or amusing and interesting, that did not happen behind the veil. As I have tried to show in other chapters even shopping and *shikar* expeditions, considered strictly outdoor occupations, took place behind the veil.

Milestones in a Child's Life

X

I n life behind the veil, ceremonies were the chief amusement, and preparations for them provided the only occupation for leisured ladies. Therefore, not only seasonal events and weddings, but any event was seized upon as an occasion for merrymaking. The birth of a child was heralded by the *Azaan*, this is the call to prayer, and as this is heard only at five fixed times of the day, the neighbours hearing it at any other time, knew that a child had been born in the vicinity. After this, words of prayer were whispered into the child's ear; these were known as *Azaan* and *Iqamat*. Each of these phrases were recited in the child's ear by the oldest male relation present; this can be likened to the Christian baptism. After this initial religious ceremony was over, the womenfolk gave themselves up to secular joyous celebration. Singing girls, known as *mirasans*, would gather together, and sing songs congratulating the parents and grandparents, and wishing joy and prosperity to the new-born child. These songs are known as *zachagirian*, and maintain a high place among the popular folk songs.

On the seventh, fourteenth or twenty-first day after the child is born, the naming ceremony, known as *aqiqa*, takes place. On this day, the child's head is shaved, and the hair weighed against silver, then silver of equal weight is distributed among the poor Two goats are also sacrificed, and the meat distributed to the poor. The naming is done by opening the Quran and taking the first letter on the first page, and selecting a name beginning with that letter. This is not obligatory, and most people who want greater freedom in naming their baby do not do this but just choose a name according to their own liking.

The barber who shaved the child's head on this occasion was generally an old retainer of the family and was richly rewarded for performing this ceremony. The custom was that his *thal*, that is the tray he brought with him carrying his razors, etc., was filled with money, with every male member of the family contributing something. This ceremony is followed by a grand feast, and in the case where it is a first child, and the family can afford it, the feasting might continue for several days and include dancing, etc. But even people of modest means sacrifice a goat and distribute meat. This is considered essential.

Six weeks rest was prescribed for mothers, right after the birth of a child; during this period, oil massages were given, tonic baths taken, and special exercises done; all this helped ladies to regain their figures. They were given especially nourishing foods; sweetmeats made out of dried fruits, rich in vitamins, figured largely in their menus. Therefore, although women in those days had many more babies than the modern woman does, they did not lose their health, strength, or figures.

The end of this period was marked by a party which was known as the *chilla*. Sometimes the *aqiqa* and *chilla* were combined, but generally the *aqiqa* took place earlier and was more of a man's ceremony. On this day, that is, the day of the *chilla*, the mother, especially if it is the first baby, is dressed as gorgeously as on her wedding day. She would put on all her jewels, sprinkle *afshan* and *chamki* on her hair, and redden her finger and toe-nails like a bride. She would then be taken into the garden for the first time since the birth of her child; this ceremony is known as 'showing the stars'. The young mother is taken out, surrounded by her friends who carry a sword over her head to ward off the evil eye; after this she is brought back and seated in the drawing-room, and fruits are put on her lap, the significance being that may she always be fruitful. Then a tray with a variety of dishes on it, is placed before her and she is made to take a little of each — this is supposed to establish tolerance in the child to all food.

When the child is about six months old, another ceremony takes place. This is known as *khir khilai* or *namak chashi*. It marks the occasion when the child has the first taste of solids. This is exclusively a woman's ceremony. All the ladies gather together, the mother and the child are both dressed up for the occasion, and the mother is seated in the centre of the drawing-room with the baby on her lap. Before her is placed a silver tray with a small silver plate with *firni* (a sort of rice pudding). The grandmother, or some other elderly member of the family, takes a tiny spoon of the rice pudding and places it on the tongue of the child; after this, there is *nichhawar*, that is touching the forehead of the child with money and putting it aside for distribution to the poor. The child also receives many presents on this occasion; there is singing of songs and congratulations and good wishes as on the occasion of the *aqiqa*, and then the party disperses.

The first and subsequent birthdays were also occasions for merrymaking. A complete record of the child's height each year is kept by tying a knot on a silken cord; the word birthday in Urdu got its name from this ceremony; it is called the *salgirah*, meaning the 'yearly knot'. On every ceremonious occasion, *laddoos*, that is a special kind of sweet which has the same place in our ceremonies as cakes have in western feasts, were made and distributed to friends and relations. The traditional age at which the child started schooling was supposed to be four years, four months, and four days. It was an occasion for celebration as well, and known as *maktab*, meaning 'The begining of school'.

Unlike *aqiqa* and *khir khilai*, *maktab* is a ceremony which takes place before a gathering of men. Women gather in the house also, but the actual ceremony takes place before men. The child is presented with a silver slate, a silver pen, a silver inkpot, and a beautifuly printed copy of the first chapter of the Quran. He is then seated on a *masnad*, in the centre of the drawing-room, and the *takhti*, (slate), *kalam* (pen), and *dawat* (inkpot), are all placed before him. Next to him sits a well-known scholar or, as often happens, a member of the family renowned for his piety and scholarship. He makes the child hold the pen in his hand, dip it into the inkpot and write the

The *Bismillah* ceremony

prayer that a Muslim always utters before undertaking any work, i.e., *Bismillah-Hirrahman-Nirrahim* (I begin in the name of God, Most Merciful and Forgiving). He also makes him recite in a most sonorous voice the words of the Quran known as *Iqra Bisme Rabbika,* meaning 'Read in the name of thy Lord...' This is the first line that was revealed to the Holy Prophet in the cave of Hira. As it is recited in a very sonorous manner, it is most impressive and leaves in the heart of the child a great impression of the grandeur of the words of the Quran. After this portion of the ceremony is over, the child is garlanded with flowers. Then he stands up, bows to all the guests present, and goes into the *zenana* where he is kissed and congratulated by all the womenfolk.

It was customary in the past to begin the education of at least half a dozen poor children along with the education of one's own child, and thus the *maktab* of those poor children also took place with the child of the house. From the next day, they all began attending classes with a private tutor in the house itself; they read the Quran, which they generally finished at the age of seven years or even earlier; they learned calligraphy, a lost art now, but in those days, years were spent in trying to teach children to write beautifully, for great importance was attached to good handwriting. In opulent houses, teachers, known as *khush nawees,* were engaged for the sole purpose of teaching the children how to write. The writing was practised on a wooden slate covered with soft earth on which the child etched out his letters, and the children spent whole mornings doing just this. Of course, education in those days meant achievement of culture, not mere hustling through examinations for the purpose of earning a living. Now after the *maktab,* the child goes straight on to a nursery school of the western type, but even now he is taught to read the Quran at home by a private tutor. When he finishes the Holy Book, a ceremony known as *nashrah* is held. On this occasion, also, the child is seated on a *masnad* against a cushion in the middle of the drawing-room. If it was a boy's *nashrah,* the ceremony would be held amongst the men, and if a girl's, amongst the women. On this occasion, there would be placed before the child a silver or an ivory or sandalwood *rehl,* (it is a kind of stand to hold the Quran) with the Quran on it wrapped in a beautiful cloth of gold called *juzdan.* The tutor would be sitting proudly next to the child. When all the guests would have assembled, the child would be asked to open the Holy Book and to read out a verse from *Sura-i-Alam Nashrah;* amidst hushed silence, the child's voice, trilling like a bird, resounds in the room. After the verse is finished there is murmur of applause; perhaps some friend or relative would ask the child to read out a verse or two more to test his knowledge of the Book, and he would do so. After this, he would be garlanded with flowers, and he would get up and pay respects, first to the tutor, and then to all the relations; then he, and more than him, the tutor, would receive congratulations.

The position of the tutor being one of very great respect in the household, he would not be rewarded obviously by friends and relatives present, as was done in the case of the barber, but a most heavily embroidered *chugha* (cloak), together with extremely

Sarvath, completing
the Holy Quran *(Nashrah)*

Guests at the ceremony

beautiful pieces of suiting, would be brought on a silver tray, alongwith a purse of Rs. 500 to Rs. 1,000 and most humbly presented to him by the father of the child, with many thanks for the trouble he had taken in initiating his son to the mysteries of learning. Phraseology used on this occasion would be something like: 'I, the father, only brought him into the world, but it is you who have made him an *Insan* (a man) by giving him the light of learning.'

In the past this occasion also signified the beginning of secondary education, and a couple or more tutors would generally be engaged, and the boy would be taught *Sarf-o-Nahv* (grammar and prosody) of the Persian and Arabic languages, philosophy, history, and even medicine, which were considered part and parcel of a gentlman's education. Riding, shooting, archery, etc., were also considered essential, and were taught by experts. Nearly every educated young man tried his hand at poetry, at one stage or another, and secured the patronage of some well-known poet of the time. At every stage of his education his tutor was shared, and the benefit of the expert's learning extended to the sons of less fortunate friends and relatives.

A girl's education after the *Nashrah* did not follow the same line. In most respectable households the learning of the Quran was considered sufficient for girls. After this, her time was taken up in learning the more feminine accomplishments like needlework, sewing, cooking, etc. Needlework was considered the most important for girls, no matter to what class of society they belonged. From plain sewing to the most exquisite embroidery with gold and silver thread and lace-making was taught to girls, and for

Sarvath with her
father after the
Nashrah ceremony

this purpose, seamstresses were engaged. Cooking was also considered essential, and here also skills ranged from plain cooking to the preparation of the most delicious sweeets, preserves and pickles. Ladies took pride in acquiring a reputation for making certain dishes remarkably well; for example, one was noted for her preserves, while another lady would take pride that no one else's *biryani* (rice with meat) had the flavour as that cooked by her; *halwas* would be the speciality of the other, and *lauz* the *piece de resistance* of someone else. Besides cooking and sewing, the girls learned dyeing, printing, starching and other useful arts.

No drudgery was involved in learning these things, for as in the case of the boys who had half a dozen other boys to study with, the girls also had a dozen other girls to share these activities. In opulent households, with nearly every daughter, two to four servant girls, known as *chhokris*, were brought up also, who were trained in all the household arts and were eventually sent with the girls as personal attendants on their marriage.

In fact, they learned through what is now known as the project method, though at that time Froebel and Montessori had not been heard of even in Europe or America. They learned cooking by doing play-cooking known as *hund-kulia*, and learned all that was to be learned of household management and the intricate social etiquette by playing with dolls. Mothers and aunts realized the educational value of such play and encouraged, advised and supervisied it. Dolls' marriages were arranged in which girls imitated, in the minutest details, all the ceremonies, and observed all the customs attendant on a real wedding. Any omission or solecism was commented upon by their elders; in this manner the girls learned what was expected from them in the all-important role of a hostess. But that was not all; as the girls made all their doll's trousseau themselves and these were displayed at the wedding, it provided them with the incentive for learning exquisite embroidery and stitching, as well as a good deal about grown-up fashions and styles. Because of its educational value, no expense was begrudged, and a doll's marriage was almost as elaborate an affair as a real one. It also served to amuse the ladies who seized upon every occasion for distraction.

Deportment played a great part in the education of a girl; they were taught how to wear their clothes, how to carry themselves, how to sit, how to get up, how to offer *pan* or sweets or to accept them from elders, how to receive the same from servants or a younger person, and what was suitable to a lady's behaviour and what was considered unsuitable. She was taught unobtrusively that most difficult of all things — good taste: what perfumes a lady could use, to what extent a lady could apply make-up and where to draw a line, and what was considered smartness and where it degenerated into showy cheapness; all these things girls learned from mothers, aunts and grandmothers. At the time when Moghul culture was at its height, and for many long years after it, prosody and versification were part and parcel of people's education. Girls were not taught, like boys, to versify, yet they got to learn it from their brothers and cousins, and it was not unusual in most respectable households for women to be able to compose poetry, and nearly all of them knew how to appreciate and assess verse. A girl was considered to have reached a marriageable age when she had attained proficiency in all these accomplishments, and the same criteria was applied to boys. This sort of personal education is not possible now and, with very few exceptions, boys and girls all go to school as in any other part of the world; much is gained, no doubt, but something is also lost.

In describing the pattern of education in detail, I have omitted to mention a few more ceremonies that marked various achievements and occasions in a child's life until he or she reached the age of maturity.

One of these was *kan-chhedan*. That is when the ears of a little girl were pierced so that she could wear earrings. On this occasion she would be dressed in brightly coloured clothes, almost like a little bride, and her first pair of earrings would be put on her ears. The actual piercing of the earlobes would be done a few days before in the presence of a few close relatives. The party would be when the girl's ears had healed and a pair of earrings could be put on her little ears.

Roza kushai, that is when the child kept the first fast, was also marked with a ceremony. The age at which a child was allowed to keep the first fast ranged from seven to twelve years, according to the physique and strength of the child. The seventeenth or the twenty-seventh day of Ramadan (the month of fasting) was generally chosen for the child to keep the first fast. The child would have a few friends with him right from early morning to keep his mind occupied, but the rest of the guests would begin arriving a couple of hours before *Iftar*.

That day the child would be exhorted to be very good, to say all his or her prayers meticulously, and to try to do as many good deeds as he or she could; moreover, he or she was not to be rude or get into a temper, and so forth. As the time for *iftar* drew near, the child would go and have a bath, put on a new set of clothes made especially for the occasion, and then come and sit amongst the assembly. As the time of *iftar*, the breaking of the fast, drew near, decanters of iced *sherbet* would be brought and put in place, the dishes of *iftari* following. All ears would be strained to hear the *Moazzin* call the *Aazan*, which is the sign for breaking the fast. As soon as the *Aazan* was heard, the child would be handed a dried date *(chhoara)* to nibble, then a glass of *sherbet* would be put to his parched lips, which he generally drained in one gulp; then a few mouthfuls of various sweets and fruits would be given to him. Then it would be time for the *Maghrib* prayers, after which everyone would sit down to a sumptuous feast. It being the month of Ramadan, there would not be any singing or merrymaking, but sometimes the hosts would engage a *Hafiz* with a particularly good voice to recite a few verses of the Quran after dinner. This was the end of the ceremony when everybody dispersed and went home to get some sleep so as to be able to get up in time for *sehri* and prepare for the next day's fast.

The Gala
Days

XI

he two gala days amongst the Muslims are *Eid* and *Baqr Eid* with *Rajab* and *Shab-i-Barat* coming as close seconds. *Eid* is celebrated to mark the end of the month of Ramadan, and it is an occasion for great rejoicing and feasting.

Preparations for *Eid* begin a good week or ten days ahead of the actual day; it helps to pass away the last days of Ramadan, and one cannot help thinking that *Eid*, with its attendant ceremonies, was fixed just for this purpose. It is customary, almost to the point of obligation, to have new clothes for this day. The rich, no matter how many dresses they might possess, would still have yet another new costume made for this occasion; and the poor, no matter how poor they may be, will try their level best to get for themselves and their children at least one new set of clothes each for *Eid;* caps, shoes and all other accessories must also be new.

Shops renew their stocks just before the advent of *Eid* and present the same sort of look as do shops in the West at the beginning of the Christmas season.

Hectic shopping goes on in the last week before Ramadan, and the last day or two are spent in feverish activity of last-minute shopping and stitching of dresses.

Like plum pudding at Christmas, the chief dish for *Eid* is *siwayan;* this is a sort of vermicelli. It is prepared in two ways. For breakfast one has *sheer khurma,* and for midday and dinner *siwayan ka zarda* is prepared. *Sheer khurma* is prepared by boiling the vermicelli in milk with shredded dry fruit. *Zarda* is prepared by cooking vermicelli in syrup and then decorating it with coloured slivers of dry fruit and silver paper.

As *Eid* depends on the appearance of the moon, it cannot be forecast with certainty whether it will fall on the twenty-ninth or the thirtieth of the month; therefore, the last two days of Ramadan are spent in excited expectancy. On the twenty-ninth evening, no sooner does the sun go down than groups of people are seen all along the streets and on terraces and balconies, trying to spot the new moon. If the moon is seen, they know it will be *Eid* the next morning, and then immediately a happy bustle begins, last minute touches are given to clothes, and the lady of the house gets busy with the arrangements for food for the next day — all this takes one far into the night. Next morning again, everyone gets up very early, and a queue is formed outside the bathroom, for everyone must have a bath before getting ready for the *Eid* prayers. Having bathed and dressed in their newest outfits, they sit down to the traditional breakfast of *sheer khurma* and milk. After this, the men go to say their prayers. *Eid* prayers are always held in an open *maidan* outside the city; in large towns, these prayers are held in several different places; the time and places are made known by announcements the evening before. In the most central place, most of the prominent citizens, and now the President, the Prime Minister, and all the other high dignitaries of State assemble to say their *Eid* prayers. They stand shoulder to shoulder with the common man, for in Muslim prayers there is no segregation and no place is, or can be, reserved for anyone, however important he might be. Still another democratic practice is that, after the prayers everyone embraces everyone else; the servant and the master embrace with great cordiality; there is no trace of condescension or patronage in anyone's attitude on *Eid* day.

The womenfolk take advantage of the men's absence to put the house in order. In the sitting-room a large table is placed in the centre, upon which crystal or silver bowls, filled with *sheer khurma* and *zarda*, are arranged. Alongside is put the *khasdan*, full of *pans* wrapped in silver paper, and the *itrdan*, with some heavenly perfume in it. *Eid* is the great day for visiting friends, and for reunions with members of the family. Straight from the *eidgah*, men wend their way to the houses of their relatives, and in each place they are greeted in the traditional way, i.e., with a touch of *itr* on their hands, after which *pans* and *siwayan* are offered. The children receive *Eidee*, that is a gift, of money, from the relations they visit. This goes on right until the evening; everyone must visit everyone else, which results in a great deal of overlapping. Lately, to avoid this, there have been attempts to organize *Eid* reunions and receptions, but they do not have the personal touch which an

individual call possesses, and will never give way to
the custom of visiting on *Eid* day. In the past, when
there was still a Moghul court, the King held a great
darbar on *Eid*, which all the notables attended. They
were greeted in the customary manner with *itr* and
pan, and they presented *nazrana* to the ruler; there
would be orchestral music, known as *nobat* and
shadyana, while the *darbar* was in progress.

It has been an age-old custom to hold a *mela*, that is
to say a fair, the day after *Eid;* this *mela* is very
much like any fair in the West. It has the usual
attractions of merry-go-rounds, round-abouts,
hawkers, vendors, jugglers, and the rest of it. To
relieve themselves of their accumulated *Eidee* of the
day before, the children go there, and the grown-ups
also catch the infection and spend their money on
absurd purchases and join the children in eating
bhuna chana and *chat* — nowadays ice cream and
chocolates. Two days of hectic activity ends *Eid*, and
everyone breathes a sigh of relief.

The second gala day for the Muslim world is *Baqr
Eid*. This is celebrated a day after the ceremony of
Hajj is performed in Mecca. Tradition has it that this
is the day on which Hazrat Ibrahim (Abraham) tried
to sacrifice his son to prove that he loved God above
everything else, and to commemorate this act of
sacrifice, a goat or cow or sheep is sacrificed by the
Muslims. A household can sacrifice from one, to as
many as half a dozen or more, animals — one for
each member of the family. The day of *Baqr Eid* is
determined ten days or so in advance, so there is not
the same uncertain expectancy as there is on the eve
of *Eid-ul-Fitr*. It is customary to go for *Baqr Eid*
prayers before having one's breakfast, and to come

back home and sacrifice the goat, and to have a piece of the sacrificial meat roasted for breakfast. The same pattern of visiting is followed; this time, besides *itr* and *pan*, deliciously prepared *kebabs* are served at each port of call. The dinner of *Baqr Eid* day is perhaps even more lavish than the one on the day of *Eid*, with meat dominating the menu. Those who can afford to make new clothes for *Baqr Eid* as well, do so, but most people make do with those made for *Eid*, there being only a two-month interval between the two festivals.

This time, the paying of visits and merrymaking continues up till the third day of *Baqr Eid*, which is the last day on which the sacrifice can be offered. Haunches and legs of mutton are sent to friends and relations, and at the end of the festival everybody begins to feel slightly sick at the sight of meat; but this is perhaps one time in the year when the poor have their fill of meat dishes. Animals that are sacrificed are required to be in very good condition and are generally bred for the sacrifice; the result is that the meat from them is much more delicious than that available on ordinary days; this is particularly appreciated as in the East the quality of the cattle is generally very poor.

Both *Eid* and *Baqr Eid* are the months in which weddings take place because they are considered to be the auspicious months. Of course, there is no reason why there should not be marriages in other months of the year, but people mostly choose these two months for the celebration of weddings. As the interval between *Baqr Eid* and *Eid* is one of ten months, the month of *Baqr Eid* is the last month of the year during which all the marriages which are left over from the previous *Eid* are celebrated; so no sooner do the festivites of *Baqr Eid* end than marriages crowd in, bringing in another round of excitement and merriment, keeping one occupied in revelries until the advent of *Moharram* when the festivities give place to mourning.

Rajab

Not comparable to *Eid* and *Baqr Eid* in their air of festivity, yet occasions for celebration are the twenty-seventh day of *Rajab* and the fourteenth day of *Sha'baan,* known as *Shab-i-Mairaj* and *Shab-i-Barat.* The *Shab-i-Mairaj* celebrates the Holy Prophet's (peace be on him) ascension to Heaven; it is a festival of the night, unlike *Eid* and *Baqr Eid* which are day festivals. On this night, houses are lit, and *Mahfil-i-Milad* are held in houses and in public places, where the story of the Ascension is chanted, with the traditional ceremonies connected with a *Mahfil-i-Milad.* As I have said before, each festivity has its special dish, and that of *Rajab* is *zarda,* i.e., sweet rice. *Zarda* is distributed after the *Mahfil-i-Milad* in little earthen plates to friends and neighbours.

Sha'baan

The fourteenth day of *Sha'baan* is known as *Shab-i-Barat,* the Night of Fate. It is the Muslim All Souls' Day, a day for the remembrance of one's dead. It is a solemn festival — not a gay one — and, like *Rajab,* it also is a festival of the night. *Halwa,* i.e., a sort of sweet of the consistency of the Turkish *Rahat*

Lukhum, and *naan,* i.e., unleavened wheat bread, is the dish which is cooked on the day of this festival. The whole day is spent in preparing this because by sundown it should be ready for distribution. When all is ready, the *naans* are heaped on a large plate or tray, and the *halwas,* which are of two or three different kinds, are put in large china bowls, and the head of the household or a *moulvi* from the neighbouring mosque blesses these, after which they are distributed to the poor; some is sent to friends as well. Great artistic ingenuity is shown in arranging the dishes. *Halwas* are covered with silver and gold paper known as *waraq,* on which is sprinkled shredded almonds and pistachio nuts. A neat pile of *naan* is put in the centre, and two or three artistically decorated bowls with *halwa* are put around it on a silver or copper tray. It is covered with a decorated tray-cloth and sent to friends. From six in the evening until late at night, and on to the next morning, there is a constant stream of servants bringing trays of *halwa-roti.* Each tray is looked upon with interest. This making and sending of *halwas* is, of course, the least important part of the ceremonies connected with *Shab-i-Barat. Shab-i-Barat,* as I said before, is a solemn festival, and as soon as the distribution of *halwa-roti* is over, everyone sits down to chant the Quran. Incense is burned and carried to every nook and corner of the house because it is believed that this is the night when the dead visit their dear ones, and the burning of incense is connected with the ceremonies for the dead. The prayers go on right up to the middle of the night, and the pious stay up the whole night praying for their dead. This night graves are visited and

flowers and lights are put on them in remembrance of one's dead.

The solemnity of this occasion is relieved by the children, for an hour or so, with fireworks. One does not quite know why this should be so because it does not seem to be in keeping with the rest of the celebrations, but tradition has it that *Shab-i-Barat* falls on the day of the Battle of Uhad, i.e., the battle in which the Muslim refugees of Mecca alongwith the converts of Medina had put up a heroic struggle against the unbelievers of Mecca and, though they had won, the casualties had been very great. The Prophet had offered special prayers for the fallen on that occasion, and so it has become a day of prayers for the dead for all times; but, as it was an occasion of victory as well, fireworks are used to commemorate it. It seems a plausible enough explanation for the fireworks. Anyway, because of the fireworks, *Shab-i-Barat* is looked forward to by the young more eagerly than any other festival, and one notices that the grown-ups too are not at all adverse, under the pretext of amusing their children, to taking part in it, and staging, the most elaborate fireworks themselves. This side of the celebrations reminds one of Guy Fawkes Day, for the children begin collecting funds for fireworks with the same avidity as children in England collect pennies for that day. One hears fireworks popping days before *Shab-i-Barat* and for several days after, also.

Mehfil-i-Milad

XII

 *Mahfil-i-Milad* is a semi-religious, semi-social function and one which is held very frequently amongst women. *Milad* means the birth of the Prophet, and *Mahfil-i-Milad* is a gathering where the story of the birth of the Holy Prophet is recited. The month of *Rabi-ul-awwal,* in which the Prophet was born, is the month in which *Mahfil-i-Milad* are held most frequently, especially in the first twelve days. The twelfth is the day of the Birth itself, and there are several big public gatherings on that day; so those who want to be quite sure that all their guests come, do not choose the twelfth as the date for holding the *milad* in their houses. They choose an earlier or a later date, for people having so many other places to go on the twelfth day may not be able to attend every function.

If it is to be a big gathering, printed invitations are sent out. The room in which the *milad* is to take place, or the marquee that has been put up for the occasion, is decorated with great care; festoons and paper chains are hung on doors and windows;

couplets in praise of the Prophet are tastefully embroidered and painted, and hung on the walls; if the function is to be held at night, coloured lights are arranged for. On the floor beautiful carpets are spread and in the centre a *takht* covered with the richest carpet is placed. Those who will read the story of the *milad* sit on this *takht*. In front of them is placed a *rehl,* that is a stand for the books. *Gulab-pash* and flower vases are placed on either side of the *rehl,* and sweet-smelling sticks and incense are burned throughout the ceremony; little trays holding these being dotted all over the room. The guests begin coming in at the specified time; this is generally at three or five in the afternoon or at seven-thirty in the evening. They seat themselves on the carpeted floor and are served *pan.* When all the guests have gathered, those who are to take part in the reading move up to the dais. Sometimes professional readers are engaged, but more often these are friends of the hostess, for being able to recite the *milad* in the accepted manner is one of the accomplishments ladies with good voices cultivate. Young girls begin to take part in reading the *milad* from the age of seven or so. The *milad* is read partly in prose and partly in verse; the prose portions are read by the lady who is considered the most learned among the party. In narrating the verse portions, two or three others join in, and the singing portions are chanted by the entire chorus. The sound of a *milad* being read is very effective, especially the portions in which the entire audience joins in. The culmination of the whole ceremony, and the most impressive portion of it is the reading of the *salaam.* It is very similar to the *Hallelujah Chorus* in the *Messiah.*

Everyone gets up when the *salaam* is being chanted and takes up the refrain which means *Peace be on you, the Prophet of God*. This is repeated after every three or four lines of poetry; the persons reading the *milad* alone recite the preceding lines, the audience only joins in the refrain; the effect is like that of the rise and fall of waves, and one cannot listen to it, even if one does not understand it, without being profoundly moved. *Gulab* is sprinkled while this is going on and *itr* is handed around as the audience sits down. All this is done for the well-known reason that a fragrant atmosphere contributes very much towards a feeling of exaltation.

After the *salaam*, a few more pieces are read and then the ceremony is ended with the reading of *munajat;* this is a prayer in verse for all present. It is also a very moving part of the ceremony. In fact, the whole of the ceremony of the *Mahfil-i-Milad*, more than any other religious ceremony, is saturated with symbolism and is consequently, very satisfying to the emotions. This accounts for its great popularity among the ladies, for the *milad* is held not only during the month of *Rabi-ul-awwal*, but on every auspicious occasion and on any conceivable pretext, for instance, moving into a new house, returning from a long journey, success of an enterprise, etc. At the completion of the *milad*, sweets are distributed in most attractive little parcels of coloured paper, tied with gold and silver tinsel. Those who can afford it, distribute sweets on glass, crystal or even silver plates, tied with gaily coloured silk handkerchiefs. If the ceremony has been in the afternoon, tea is served; if in the evening, dinner follows, but not necessarily. It is matter of no reproach at all if a *milad* ends with just a distribution of sweets and cold drinks. Nowadays, particularly, this is what happens.

Koondas-An
Interesting
Story

XIII

oondas are a ceremony performed by Muslim ladies which definitely savour of Hindu influence. As a matter of fact, the story of the origin of this custom is a most interesting one. It shows how ingenious the female mind can be in thinking out ways and means to humiliate a hated rival.

The name of Nur Jehan conjures up visions of beauty, charm and romance. Her life story deserves the caption, 'Truth is stranger than fiction'. Born in a noble family fallen on evil days, abandoned on the wayside at birth, picked up by a caravan of kindly merchants who engaged her own mother to look after her, fortune smiles on her father once again; she rises from one position of power to another, and in the end is introduced to the court of Akbar, the richest and most famous court of the East at that time. Nur Jehan, whose name yet is Mehrunnisa, becomes a frequent visitor to the court. The sun of her beauty reaches its zenith and its rays attract the eyes of Salim, the heir to the most magnificent and wealthy throne of the East, a child of many hopes and prayers. Akbar, the Great Moghul, dreams of alliances with the turbulent and proud Rajputs. How can he allow his son to marry Mehrunnisa, the daughter of an impoverished family of Iran; all the might of the empire comes between the ill-starred lovers and separates them. Mehrunnisa is hurriedly married to a young cavalry officer and sent out to far-off Bengal, and Salim is betrothed and married, with pomp and splendour, to the daughter of the most powerful of the Rajputs, the Rana of Jodhpur. In the veins of their sons mingle Moghul and Rajput blood, and Akbar's dream of Hindu-Muslim unity seems near to realization.

But the flame in the heart of Jehangir continues to smoulder for many years. At last, Akbar dies at a ripe old age. Jehangir has now been married for fifteen years and is the father of many sons. Yet he has not forgotten the gazelle-like Persian maiden whom, in that far-off youth of his, he had met one day in the gardens of the Fatehpuri Palaces and to whom he had given two little pigeons to hold for him. One of these had flown away and Jehangir, annoyed at her carelessness, had asked what had happened. 'It flew away, sir,' she said.

'But how?' asked the prince rather irritably. 'Like this, sir', she said, letting the other one go also. No, he had not forgotten that innocent, coquettish gesture of hers.

History does not record exactly what transpired when Akbar died, but the fact is that Mehrunnisa's husband was killed trying to suppress a local rebellion and, on receipt of this news, the King ordered that Mehrunnisa be sent back to Delhi with royal honours. On her arrival at the Court, she hears

Nur Jahan, one of the most
fascinating women of
Indian history

whispers that perhaps her husband's death was not
the accident she had imagined it to be, and begins to
suspect that perhaps the Emperor had a hand in it.
For seven long years, this suspicion clouded
Mehrunnissa's mind, and she refused Salim's
supplications to become his queen. But after seven
weary years, all told twenty-two years or so of
waiting, Salim's love was rewarded and Mehrunnisa
became his wife. He called her, first, Nur Mahal the
'Light of the Palace', and then, Nur Jehan, the 'Light
of the World'. He gave not only his heart in her
keeping, but the reins of government also. His cup of
happiness was full; he needed nothing more.
But there were thorns to this rose of perfect
happiness, as there always are. Salim was now
Emperor Jehangir, and his first wife could not be
expected to submit to the insult of being supplanted
like this. She, the descendant of the proud Rajputs,
to be humiliated in this way! She thought and she
planned in many ways to bring about the downfall of
Nur Jehan. But the sun of Nur Jehan's fate had come
out of the clouds at last and was shining in full
splendour and nothing could dull its radiance. All
efforts of this proud daughter of the Rajputs to bring
her down failed. She thought and she thought, her
wounded vanity sought some means of assuaging
itself and hit upon a most ingenious plan; she staged
a most elaborate ceremony, the ceremony of offering
niaz in the name of Bibi Fatima, the Prophet's
daughter.
Now, strictly speaking, *nazar* and *niaz* are not
Islamic; food and drink dedicated in somebody's
name do not get consecrated in Islam, but by this
time a lot of Hindu influence had permeated the

Moghul court in the wake of Rajput princesses, and the idea was taking hold that anything offered in the name of a saintly person became sanctified. The Rajput queen arranged a most elaborate party to which all the ladies of the court were invited, among whom, of course, was Nur Jehan, who was seated in a place of honour, the cynosure of all eyes, being not only the King's favourite but the queen of his heart and of the realm. The Rajput Queen, too, seemed to show no resentment today, but went about happily arranging the details for the *niaz*. In an adjoining pavilion, washed with rose-water and made further fragrant by the burning of *loban* in silver and gold bowls, a milk-white table-cloth was laid; food cooked by seven ladies of highest ranks and purest of characters was to be served there. When all was ready, the Rajput Queen came into the hall where the guests were assembled and asked them to enter the pavilion where *niaz*, in the name of Bibi Fatima, the pure and noble daughter of the Prophet, was laid out. There was a stir in the hall as the ladies got up. The maids-in-waiting ran forward to hold the trains and take up their ladies' fans and *pandans*. Nur Jehan, too, adjusted the folds of her *peshwaz* and got up; all waited for Nur Jehan to lead the way but, as she took the first step towards the pavilion, her rival came forward with a most reluctant air and said, 'Madam, I am sorry, you cannot partake of this food because, it is dedicated to the name of Fatima and only those can eat it who have been married but once.' The Rajput Queen had had her revenge! Before the flower of the Moghul aristocracy, Nur Jehan had been humiliated. It had been driven home in a telling way that she might be supreme in the heart of Jehangir, but she was not his first, the rightful wife.

There is no record of how Nur Jehan took this insult, or what the reaction of Jehangir was to all this. But there are stories that, when asked for an explanation, the Rajput Queen innocently remarked that she had completely forgotten that Nur Jehan had been married before and that she had staged this dedication in all innocence; only at the last moment had it dawned on her that Nur Jehan could not eat the food.

Whatever the truth of this story may be, the fact remains that this custom, thought out by a queen to salve her wounded vanity, remained with the ladies of the Moghul court, and to this day, on the eve of a girl's marriage and many other occasions, such as on her recovery from some illness and so on, a *koonda* ceremony is held. Food is cooked in a specially cleaned and perfumed place by ladies of unblemished character and reputation. It is cooked all night and in the early hours of the morning it is laid in a room where no man can see it, and it is partaken of by seven, fourteen, or twenty-one girls, and ladies. Unmarried girls, married women and widows can partake of it, but no woman who has been married more than once can touch this consecrated food. As I said before, this is a completely unIslamic attitude as Islam enjoins a widow's remarriage and no odium whatsoever is attached to it; but this custom, as I have shown, originated in the pique of a Hindu queen, and to this day is carried out in the same way as she planned it.

But the *koondas* somehow seem to have taken the fancy of the ladies, and they have thought out many more instances when *koondas* can be held. Now

there are at least half a dozen different occasions and kinds of *koondas*, dedicated to different saintly persons. For the long life and success of a boy, a *koonda* is dedicated to Hazrat Ali.

Here again food is prepared elaborately by the ladies, but is served and eaten by men. Then there are the *koondas* held on the twenty-second of *Rajab*. Anyone at any time can decide to have a *koonda;* all that is needed is that the ceremony be dedicated to the memory of some holy person; that the food should be cooked with a great deal of elaboration, and that it should be eaten at the place where it has been cooked. The most popular *koonda* is the one held on the twenty-second of *Rajab* and dedicated to Imam Jafar Sadiq. For this *kheer* (rice pudding of a sort) and little flour cakes *(puris)* are cooked. These are then served in large earthen bowls *(koondas)* and eaten at the place of their cooking.

Koondas mean so much preparation and modern life is so hustled that fewer and fewer people care to undertake it now.

Ramadan
The Month
of Prayer

XIV

s with the Christians of old, for Muslims also the holy days of the past have become holidays of the present; but their religious origin have not deprived them of pageantry and colour. *Eid, Baqr Eid, Rajab, Shab-i-Barat*, each of these mark an occasion of religious import, and yet each is full of colour and merriment. Even Ramadan, the month of prayer, comparable to the Lent of the Catholics, brings a sort of festive atmosphere with it. Ramadan is the month in which the Muslims are enjoined to fast, and the Muslim fast is the severest imaginable. One does not eat or drink from the early hours of dawn till sunset. This, in the hot countries of the East, on long summer days, is a feat of endurance. I do not wish to enlarge upon the beneficial effects of *roza*, i.e., the training and discipline which it means, but merely to show the manner in which the holy month is observed. Food and drink being prohibited from sunrise to sunset, there is hardly any culinary activity except for the children of the household.

Those who observe the fast get up in the early hours of the morning just before dawn and have breakfast; this meal is known as *sehri,* and consists of tasty, light and nourishing foods. Some prefer to have a cold *sehri,* but in households where several people are fasting, servants get up around 3:00 a.m and begin cooking. After *sehri,* has been taken, generally no one goes to bed, but as the first rays of the sun become visible on the horizon, begin their ablutions and stand up for their early morning prayers, after which the Quran is recited loudly by those with beautiful voices, and it is most impressive to hear the sonorous Arabic words rising as a clarion call in the hushed hours of the morning. After an hour or more of prayer and of reading the Quran, the household goes to sleep. Those who can sleep late do so, others get up and go about their daily work as usual. Yet in the days of Ramadan there is an atmosphere of quietude. People do not loiter in the streets; eating places and places of amusement are closed, and the only noise one hears is the cry and play of small children.

After the midday prayers, the ladies try to while away the time by reading, writing and needlework; the thinking out and planning of the wardrobe for the coming *Eid* also provides them with plenty to do. I sometimes think that the custom of decreeing new apparel for *Eid* for everyone was only devised to give women occupation during the long Ramadan days, and to keep their minds away from thoughts of food. From five to five-thirty in the afternoon, preparations for *Iftar,* i.e., breaking the fast, begin; especially appetizing dishes are cooked and got ready to be eaten immediately after the sun goes down. A large decanter of iced *sherbet* of various juices, or milk, is placed on the table, and cold, iced fruit looks very inviting; one can hear the sizzling of delicious snacks in the kitchen and pretend to keep one's mind away from thoughts of food. As the sun goes down the call of the *Moazzin* is heard; the hour has come to break the fast. With a short prayer, thanking God for having enabled one to go through the ordeal, one nibbles at a *chhoara,* i.e., a dried date, or sliced ginger, and then thankfully drinks a couple of glasses of iced *sherbet.* A hasty sampling of the snacks follows, because *maghrib* (evening) prayers must be said, after which some sit down straight away, others after an interval, to a real good feed. But, here again, wise tradition has guarded against the temptation of over-eating. *Taraveeh* (that is extra prayers) have to be said, and one would not be able to do so loaded with too much food. After a short rest, the men go to the neighbourhood mosque to attend the *taraveeh* while the women offer the same prayers at home. The month of Ramadan is a month meant to revive the observance of all religious duties, and, to ensure this, special customs are fixed. Incorporated into the daily *taraveeh* prayer is one chapter of the Quran and, in this way by the end of the month, the whole Quran is read at least once. *Khatam taraveeh,* i.e., the day on which the Quran is completed, falls on the twenty-seventh or twenty-eighth day of Ramadan, and the mosques are lighted, and sweets distributed on that day to the poor.

It is enjoined on the Muslims to give *zakat,* i.e., two-and-a-half per cent of one's savings, to charity, and tradition has established that it is most meritorious to give *zakat* in the month of Ramadan. A very wise

way of ensuring that the Eid expenses of the poor are provided for, and on that gala day, at least, they do not look ragged.

Taraveeh prayers are generally over about midnight; some people go home and take some light refreshment and then do not get up for *sehri;* others go to sleep and then get up again for *sehri.*

On the twenty-seventh day of Ramadan, the Prophet is said to have had the first line of the Quran revealed to him, and that night, therefore, like the night of *Shab-i-Barat,* is one of prayer; it is known as *Lail-atul-Qadr,* the Sublime Night. On that night the pious are heard reciting the Quran right through and all the mosques are ablaze with light; it creates a. wonderful impression. Still more impressive is the *Juma-tul-Wida,* the last Friday of the month of Ramadan. On that day people flock to the nearest cathedral mosque of the city. The gathering at the famous cathedral Mosque of Delhi was always a magnificent spectacle. One saw nothing but a sea of humanity brought together in their single-minded devotion to their religion, standing row upon row, rich, shoulder to shoulder, with the poor, all social distinctions forgotten in the house of God. A similar spectacle is seen at the Badshahi Mosque in Lahore, and in every mosque, big or small, in the subcontinent.

After the *Juma* prayers there is a stirring *khutba,* i.e., a sermon in which the speaker, who is generally a well-known orator and a person of learning, delivers a speech. The topic of the *khutba* naturally varies from year to year, but it is always in the nature of an exhortation to better things and is delivered in a manner which brings out the conflict between the frailty of the flesh and the divine urge in human beings. It is a subject which, in the hands of an orator has a tremendous emotional appeal and a tremendous effect on the congregation.

Ramadan, the month of prayer, the month of discipline and piety, is not a dull month. It has its own peculiar appeal and charm, like that of a High Mass, in which the soul rises to heights of sublimity and inspiration.

Moharram
The Days
of Mourning

XV

ne cannot describe *Moharram* as a festival because it commemorates the most tragic event in the history of Islam; yet the days of *Moharram* have an element of dramatic, though tragic, atmosphere about them. *Moharram* commemorates the martyrdom of Hussain, the grandson of the Prophet. He and his entire family were killed after being ambushed in the desert and kept without food and water for three whole days. But a bald statement like this cannot convey the aura of tragic grandeur with which this sad incident is surrounded and the tradition of mourning that has grown around it. The fact that some of the best elegiac poetry in Persian and in Urdu has the event of Kerbala as its theme has succeeded in taking this event out of the realm of pure religious devotion and has put it into an extremely high level of literary excellence. In these elegiac poems, known as *marsias,* there is magnificent characterization, superb narration and masterly dramatic presentation of incidents. The bare bones of history have been made to live because they

have been infused with the life-blood of imagination; the dialogue and narration are equally superb, with a masterly understatement here, and just the right amount of exaggeration there.

The result of this superb presentation is that the events of Kerbala are for every Muslim a very real occurrence. The way in which this tragedy, enacted some fourteen hundred years ago, is mourned over still, is a wonderful example of what literary genius can achieve, for what would have remained in the realm of reason has been brought into the region of emotion and given a depth which artistic excellence alone is capable of.

The days of *Moharram* are observed as days of mourning with as much punctiliousness by Muslim households as the days of mourning after the death of someone near and dear. The period of mourning for Muslims is forty days, and this is the period observed for *Moharram* also, but the first thirteen days are observed with a greater rigidity. The rest of the period is a period of mourning in as much as no joyful event, such as marriage, etc., can be celebrated; otherwise there is not much difference in the ordinary routine of life. The first days, however, especially among the Shia section of the Muslim community are observed with great strictness and are full of ceremonies, and it is these ceremonies which give it that element of tragic drama about which I spoke earlier.

Imam Hussain was murdered at midday on the tenth of *Moharram*. He is believed to have arrived on the banks of the Euphrates on the third day of *Moharram*. Enemies closed in on him from the very first day and, on the seventh, he was cut off from the river, the only source of water. After three days of discussions and attempts to make the enemy see reason, Imam Hussain's followers decided to come out in the field and die fighting. One by one they came, and each sold his life dearly indeed to the enemy; the last to fall was the leader himself. After his martyrdom, the women and children were taken prisioner, their tents set on fire, and they were subjected to every indignity and humiliation that the human mind can think of — they were taken, bareheaded and manacled, through the streets of Damascus to the court of the tyrant, thrown into prison, and finally, for fear of a general uprising, released and allowed to return to Medina.

These are the incidents that are related in the superb elegies of Anis and other poets and the recitation of these is begun from the evening on which the *Moharram* moon appears on the horizon. Each day, or I should say each evening, is given over to the recitation of the event that is supposed to have occurred on that day. The first evening is devoted to the recitation of the parting of Imam Hussain from his friends and relations in Medina. Here Anis's versatile pen has drawn unforgettable pictures around this event, one of the saddest things of life — the saying of goodbye to one's friends. The second and the third of *Moharram* are given over to the description to the journey from Medina to Kerbala, the heat of the long desert day, the dust of the road, the tedium of travelling, the pleasant cool of the morning, the twilight of the evening, all are depicted in the minutest detail. Disquieting rumours, evil tidings come to Imam Hussain. Friends advise him to turn back, women are frightened, children cry human nature in all its aspects is presented through the narration. On the third night, the arrival on the banks of the Euphrates, at the place known to the ancients as Nineveh, is described; this place has henceforth been called *karb-o-bala,* the Place of Agony and Disaster, by the Muslims.

There is an air of doom about it all; Imam Hussain has come to meet his fate. He goes through the formality of trying in every way to save himself, but it is only pure formality — the feeling of doom permeates the entire description. There are magnificent descriptive passages showing the contrast between the pompous arrival of the enemy's armies and Imam Hussain's straggling band of seventy-two. The contrast between right and wrong is brought out in a way in which only a genius could have done. The peace, the single-mindedness, the entire devotion in the hearts and minds of Imam Hussain's followers stand out in contrast to the feeling of conflict in the minds of the enemy's hordes. The weakness of the flesh, the flicker of the spirit, the love of wealth, the stifling of the voice of conscience, all these emotions are shown to be raging in the hearts of those thousands upon thousands of horsemen, swordsmen, spearsmen and bowmen that are pitted against one solitary unarmed figure. Out of that multitude of unbelievers comes one lone person whose voice of conscience would no longer let him rest. Hur, commander of a whole battalion, sees light at the eleventh hour, and breaks away; along with him come his son and one devoted slave; they come from the side where there is certain victory and worldly gain to join the side where there is certain and immediate death, but which is upholding the banner of right.

Now the stage is all set; the last word has been spoken, the last argument finished. In the tents of Imam Hussain children are crying with hunger and thirst, the situation has become untenable; there is nothing left for the men but to go out and die, for the misery of the women and children cannot be endured. The fateful morning of the tenth day of *Moharram* dawns; every one of the small band is eager to die for they firmly believe that with death in a cause as noble as this will come the crown of martyrdom, the joys of Paradise, the rewards of the just, and all are eager to be the first to secure the prize. One by one they go, never to come back, and soon Imam Hussain is left with his half-brother, Abbas, his son, Akbar, his nephew, Qasim, and the two teen-aged boys of Zainab, his sister. He wants to go himself to the field of battle, for it is he the enemy are after, but his group would not hear of it. It would be a matter of everlasting shame for them if they were to allow him to die while there was still breath in them. So, one by one they seek permission and are reluctantly allowed to go. The two youngsters of Hazrat Zainab, whose mother, since the night before had been urging them not to fail her by showing any reluctance or cowardice in the field of battle, are the first to set forth, and they do not fail or falter in their task. Sons of a brave mother, they die bravely. Qasim, son of Imam Hussain's elder brother, betrothed to his daughter has had his marriage celebrated only the night before, with death already upon them; he drinks the cup of martyrdom leaving his day-old bride a widow. Abbas, the most heroic of the heroes of Kerbala, goes next. He, the son of Ali, the only one in the prime of manhood, battles his way right up to the banks of the river, fills the *mashk* (the leather water sack), slings it on to his shoulder, and speeds his horse to return quickly to the camp in order to assuage the thirst of Sakina, the four-year old daughter of Imam Hussain, who has been gasping for breath because not a drop of water has touched her parched throat for three whole days. But alas! the bulging sack of water is an easy target and the enemy horsemen aim their arrows at it. He quickly shields the sack,, exposing his chest as a target; he fights desperately, like a stag at bay, trying to get nearer and nearer to the tent. It is almost in sight; he is almost there, when a sword falls on the shoulder on which the *mashk* is slung. With a movement as quick as lightning, he slings it on to the other shoulder and speeds his horse to further action; but alas! another sword blow severs that arm also; he makes a desperate attempt to clutch the sack in his teeth, but all hope is destroyed, as an arrow pierces the leather and the water begins trickling away. Water secured through so much effort, water as precious as blood, trickles away, and with it passes the last breath of life from Abbas' body. He falls from his horse and dies; perhaps he did not want to return without water and face the dismay and disappointment of the children.

There are dozens upon dozens of elegies that describe this desperate fight for water by Hazrat Abbas. The poignancy, the heroism, the deep and tender devotion of this man of iron for that little girl, are all brought out. The presentation and delineation of Hazrat Abbas' character is perhaps the best of Anis' efforts, and no effort of his can be said to be

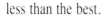

less than the best.

The events of Kerbala have been narrated in a rising crescendo of tragedy. After Abbas' death comes that of Akbar, the eighteen year old son of Imam Hussain, the pride of his heart, strength of his old age, heir of the noble tradition, the image of the Prophet, hope of the future; his mother is the daughter of the Kasras of Persia, so in Akbar's veins, flows the imperial blood of Iran as well. To let such a son die in the cause of truth requires courage indeed; it does not come easy, and the description by Anis of this tearing of Imam Hussain's heart by his own hands, because he believed in something greater than life itself, is again one of his great achievements. After the death of Akbar, one would have thought that the cup of sacrifice was full, that nothing further could be demanded; but no; there was yet one more shaft left. There was the six-month old baby, Asghar, who was dying of thirst. His mother thought that perhaps the enemy would have mercy on him, so Imam Hussain carried him out to the enemy and asked for water to be given to the baby; the reply was a well-aimed arrow at the innocent parched throat.

So, as the midday sun rose to its zenith, Imam Hussain alone was left, a majestic figure on his wounded charger, the dead all around him. The last farewell, the grandeur of this solitary fighter for the cause of righteousness, the hopelessness and the greatness of his mission; and then his death, the loot, the indignities and the misery of his family and the return 'home' are described. How well all this is done by Anis can only be appreciated by those who can read Urdu.

All these incidents are read one by one, day after day and night after night during *Moharram*. On the seventh night is described the betrothal of Qasim to Kubra, Imam Hussain's daughter; on the ninth, the waiting for the doom; on the tenth morning, the holocaust; on the eleventh, the looting of the tents and the taking of prisoners; on the twelfth, the weary trudge to Damascus; on the thirteenth the burying of the dead; and then, at intervals of a week or a few days, the various incidents during the period of imprisonment; and on the fortieth day, the return to Medina.

These recitations of the elegies are not mere reading; they are read with a great deal of form and ceremony. Here again, the Shias, the more devout sect of the Muslims, are punctilious about the observance of the ceremonies; whereas the more puritanical sect of the Muslims, who do not believe in ritualism and observances, are not so particular. In *Moharram*, women dress in black, take off their jewellery, abjure perfume and avoid make-up. New clothes are not bought, nor any work, such as building of houses or moving into new ones, undertaken. No weddings or other ceremonies take place, but it should not be imagined that, because of it, these are days of unrelieved monotonous grief. Grief and sorrow there is, but it has a ritualistic setting which relieves it of boredom and somehow makes one feel as if one is participating in a tragic drama lasting several days.

Women certainly wear only black, but do not imagine for a moment that they just wrap themselves up thoughtlessly in any six-yard piece of unrelieved black cloth. Some do just that, but only those who are elderly and of a very religious turn of mind; the younger ones think out their wardrobe for *Moharram* days ahead with almost as much care as the *Eid* wardrobe. They have to confine themselves necessarily to the two colours, black and white, but the ingenious female mind can think out a dozen permutations and combinations even in these two colours. Saris or *dupattas* are trimmed with black sequins, edged in contrasting colours; white polka dots on black and vice-versa, stripes, checks, and many other prints give a variety to the wardrobe. Jewellery is not worn, that is to say that gold ornaments are taken off, but smart young things sport jet earrings with rings to match, and onyx and other semi-precious stones are pressed into service on this occasion. Black shoes and bag complete the ensemble.

Pan is not supposed to be eaten during this time because it reddens the lips, but as *pan* eaters have a habit of chewing and would be lost without something to chew, an elaborate concoction of spices is made instead. This is known as *gota,* not to be confused with the *gota* that is the gold lace used for trimming clothes. This *Moharram ka gota* is made out of cinnamon seeds, cardamom, shredded dried coconut, raisins and almonds. It is prepared very elaborately. Shredded coconut is dyed in various bright colours; acacia nuts are wrapped in silver paper and mixed with the rest of the spices. Having spent so much time and trouble in preparing it, naturally opportunity is sought to display one's handiwork; therefore, the custom is to exchange *gota*. Small satin pouches are sewn and *gota* is put in them, and these are sent as presents to friends.

Like every Muslim feast day, *Moharram* has its characteristic dish; this is known as *halim* or *khhichra*. It is cooked with five or seven different kinds of grain and meat put together. It is always cooked in enormous quantities and is left to simmer all night. This is distributed to the poor on the seventh and tenth days of *Moharram;* it is also customary to distribute *sherbet,* i.e., sweetened iced drinks. On those occasions when *Moharram* falls during days of scorching heat, this is truly a boon. This distribution of *sherbet* is known as *sabil;* distribution of *sherbet* may be done on all the ten days, or only on the seventh, ninth, and tenth days, or only on the tenth, depending on the means and piety of various households. The distribution of *sherbet* also has a ritual; little children are dressed in green and given water-sacks, and told to go out on the road and give cold drinks to hot and weary travellers. They do so, generally to the accompaniment of some appropriate verse saying that the drinks are being given in memory of him who died thirsting for water.

Moharram is the only festival of the Muslims in which symbolic representations are made. This is definitely an unIslamic thing and is a result of the contact with India and Persia. They, however, are extremely picturesque, and do help, as a symbolic representation always does, in making the whole affair much more concrete. A sort of mock battle, funeral and burial is staged. On the seventh day of *Moharram,* the *duldul* comes out — a horse, richly bridled and saddled, together with flags, drums, shields, etc., and men to stage a mock fight. On the ninth night and on the tenth afternoon, the *tazias* are taken out. These are tomb-like structures made in the days when kings and courts existed of gold and silver, but now mostly of bamboo and paper; they look extremely decorative.

One is not quite clear as to what *tazias* are supposed to represent. They do not represent a funeral because they are made in the form of tombs. Tradition has it that one of the Shahs of Persia fell ill during one *Moharram* and could not visit Kerbala, as was his custom each year. He, therefore, had the replica of all the tombs made, and these were brought to him in a procession in lieu of visiting the shrines themselves. Since then, it has become the custom to do this every year; this seems a plausible enough explanation.

These *tazias* are made by different guilds; even now the guild system exists to some extent in the East; and the *tazias* of each guild represent the craft that they excel in. For instance, I have seen the *tazias* of *malis*, i.e., gardeners, made entirely of green grass and leaves; those of *chooriwalas*, i.e., bangle-makers, made entirely of bangles; those of cotton weavers made entirely of cotton wool, and so forth. The *tazias* are carried on the shoulders of the people to the accompaniment of a dirge-like recital of *marsias* and *nohas*, lighted torches, banners and shields. They start from *Imam baras*, that is places where *tazias* are kept during the period of their construction, follow a prescribed route, and come back again to the *Imam baras*. This happens in those cities where on the ninth night a procession of *tazias* is taken out. In other cities going over the traditional route, they reach the bank of some river, or a certain place, where they are collected and demolished.

Besides *tazias* on the tenth afternoon, come out the procession of *taboots,* i.e., the actual representation of the funeral. The procession of *tazias* are followed by the common populace and is, on the whole, a rowdy, noisy sort of procession, accompanied by *naqarahs,* looking at which no one would think that it was in commemoration of a sad event.

Taboots, on the other hand, are followed by the learned and more respectable elements of society. They are not accompanied by music but by the doleful recital of *marsias,* giving it a very solemn air.

The ten days of *Moharram* for an ordinary uneducated person are a sort of fete. *Tazias* are made, not only by the Shias but by the Sunnis also, and in the days of Hindu-Muslim accord even Hindus participated in their construction. Inhabitants of each locality take part in the construction of the *tazia* of that area. While the processions of *tazias* are watched by Sunnis and Shias alike. The educated class of both the Sunnis and Shias do not take part in actually constructing the *tazias* or in carrying them in the procession, nor does the ritualistic reading of *marsias,* known as *majlis,* take place in the houses of Sunnis. *Majlis* are the focus of all social life for the Shias in the days of *Moharram;* they take place every day for the first ten days in the houses of well-to-do people and in various public places. There are sometimes three to four *majlis* on the same day. In a well-to-do Shia household, it would be unheard of to let the entire *Moharram* pass without having at least one *majlis* — it is done as a social obligation.

Majalis are organized very much like any other ceremonious gathering; beautiful carpets are spread out in the largest room of the house, and cushions put in various places for guests to recline on. The *masnad* that is an extra rich carpet, is placed in the centre of the room for the *marsia-khwan* to sit on and recite the *marsias*. *Pandan, ugaldan,* and *hookah* are put at convenient intervals for the guests. Nowadays electricity has done away with the elaborate preparations for light; formerly, the whole room would be glimmering with rows and rows of flickering candles or huge oil-lamps. After the recitation is over, *sheerni,* i.e., sweets, are distributed to the guests present and, of course, *sherbet* is served as well as tea.

On the eighth night, *hazri* is given. This consists of *sheermal, kebab,* and a slice of cheese. In some households the guests stay on for dinner; after the *majlis.* The *majalis* are, as I have said before, a social affair, and in fact this is the only social event during the *Moharram* days.

Like Ramadan, the days of prayer which have a religious grandeur about them, *Moharram* has its atmosphere of tragic splendour.

The Rains Came

XVI

t is difficult to convey to Western readers what the coming of the rains mean to the people of the Indo-Pakistan subcontinent. It can only be likened to the advent of spring in the West, when the bare and dormant earth comes to life again; much the same happens with the coming of the rains in this country. For three months before the rains, there is intense heat; all things die or are dried up; one does not see a blade of grass or a green leaf on the trees, for most trees in this country shed their leaves to store their moisture at this time. The heat is simply suffocating — to go out of doors after ten o'clock in the morning is impossible, and it is only after the sun has set that people can be seen out and about in the streets again. In short, the three months, i.e., from mid-April to mid-July, people do not live — they merely exist. Even the flimsiest garment seems constricting; no food is edible, only ice-cold drinks. As these weary months draw to an end, the advent of rain is eagerly awaited, and all eyes are turned towards the sky to detect even a speck of cloud. The air is sniffed to

detect any moisture in it; day after day passes in expectation and in agony, and then — the rains come!

They come in heavy showers, with thunder and lightning, and it pours for days on end. The parched earth drinks up the mositure, the dry trees drain every drop and soon there are green leaves and green grass, and purple clouds, and life becomes possible again. The strain of heat removed, people's thoughts turn immediately towards enjoyment, and, strange as it might seem, the traditional forms of amusement, at this time, are picnics and outings. *Sawan*, i.e., the first month of the rains, is a joyous month, and as usual, has its own special form of enjoyment. To go out of the city into villages, to large fruit gardens, or to parks surrounding historical places, is the thing to do in *sawan*. Unlike Western picnics, cooked food is not taken; rather, all the paraphernalia of cooking and the raw stuff is carted to the place of the outing, and there, under the trees, delectable savouries are cooked and served piping hot.

The older and more industrious members of the party are cooking under one tree while the younger and more frivolous ones string a swing to the bough of another and are singing with the abandon of larks, keeping time with the gentle swaying of the swing. There are special folk-songs for these occasions which describe the joyous scenes of *sawan*, the coming to life of the earth, the getting together of friends, and the exuberance surrounding everything. It also has its pathos; girls married far away from home recall their childhood friends and the good times they had with them swinging and singing songs. So the young married ones sing these wistful songs as they get the food ready for the members of their party. These picnics generally last two or three days, or even a week.

Most rich families had fruit gardens and country houses outside their city dwellings where they went regularly for outings. On the outskirts of Delhi or Lahore, even to this day, there are these beautiful mango gardens with *bara daries,* i.e., pavilions for resting, cooking and so forth. There are delightful *bara daries* through which the water cunningly flowed and came out in cascades, and in which there were little niches that held shimmering lights during the night and flowers during the day. All is in ruins now, but they testify to the joy of living that the people of that era possessed.

While the common folk relied on their own resources to provide singing and music, musicians and singing girls accompanied the Nawabs and noblemen in the past, and in the quiet of the countryside and in the peace of the forest, the sounds of revelry and gaiety rang out for days.

Even today, many families have mango gardens which are the favourite spots for picnics. Such elaborate outings are, no doubt, confined to the rich, but no matter how poor a family they go out, at least for a day, when the rains come. No matter if they do not own private gardens, the beautiful grounds surrounding the lovely Moghul buildings are theirs, and when the rains come, in every nook and corner of the Qutub Minar or the Shalamar gardens, can be seen groups of happy people singing, cooking and enjoying themselves.

The first *sawan* outing after there has been a marriage in the family is an occasion for more than the usual merriment and fun. The bride dresses in a greyish purple *gharara,* a light green *kurta,* and *dupatta* — the hues that blend most with the landscape of grey clouds and green trees. The groom also puts on a green *kurta,* and both wear garlands of flowers around their necks and around their wrists. Swings are suspended from the trees and the young couple take their seats on them; the swing-board might be of brightly coloured wood or even of pure silver; the cord is of brightly coloured silk. The swing is pushed to and fro by friends and young relations to the accompaniment of endless jokes and quips. *Sawani* is sent by the girl's parents to her, and her husband. This would consist of the inevitable set of clothes together with *mehndi* and flowers and other toilet accessories.

The mother-in-law too, would always present the daughter-in-law with a set of new clothes for *sawan;* these clothes, while being of very bright hues and of extremely attractive styles, would not be expensive but the kind that would stand rough wear and sitting about on the grass, Young girls would get themselves at least a new *dupatta,* and would certainly dye all their old ones in the bright new shades, for in summer it is impossible to wear anything but white or very pale colours. With the cooler days after the rains, bright hues come back in vogue — emerald green, orange, primrose yellow, and purple are the colours most favoured in this season.

In the naming of colours also ladies showed much ingenuity and imagination. Colours were likened to flowers, fruits and even vegetables. Every shade had a different name, while pink was *gulabi* (rose), a paler shade with a tinge of mauve was *piazi* (the colour of the inner layer of the onion peel). Shocking pink was *tarboozi*, (the inside of a water melon), and bright red was *gulnar* (the flower of the pomergranate); a lush pink was *shaftalu* (peach), shades of yellow ranged from *narangi* (orange) and *zaffarani* to *jogia* (yellow) and *champai* the pale gold of the lotus bud. Older women wore the more sophisticated colours, such as *badami* (almond), *khaki* (weed green) and *kafuri* (egg-white). For winter were the *sardai* colours, i.e., *honey*, *dew melon* — warm colours to suit the season.

Dyeing *dupattas* in the *barsati* shades and putting *mehndi* on their fingers form the chief occupations of young girls at this time of the year. *Mehndi*, at this season, is supposed to be of a brighter hue than at any other time, so it is the time to colour lotus-like fingers with the 'red of the henna trees'; The girls pluck and dry and keep the *mehndi* of this season to be used at different times of the year.

Like dress, food also is different at this time of the year. It is more tasty and cooked in an appetizing manner to coax jaded appetites. Fruits are plentiful and are eaten a good deal. This is the time when the famous mangoes are plentiful, and most of the *sawan* parties take place in the mango gardens where one eats mangoes galore. As a matter of fact, there is a regular competition to see who eats the most. Besides, there are many varieties of melon and watermelons available. These are iced and chilled and made into *sherbet*. A delicious fruit at this time of the year is called the *jamun*. It looks like olives and has a somewhat similar taste; *lychee* is another fruit which is plentiful at this time. In short, nature is lavish with her gifts during this season and man takes full advantage of it.

Music

XVII

he strains of music were constantly heard behind the veil. Every joyous occasion demanded music: weddings, picnics, banquets and innumerable children's ceremonies were all celebrated with songs and dances. The group of singing and dancing women known as *mirasans,* were the indispensable entertainers behind the veil. They were sent for on every occasion, and whenever the ladies were in a mood for a little frolic and entertainment. As a matter of fact, *mirasans* were, for all practical purposes, part of the household staff. They did not stay on the premises but were attached to the household as firmly as the residents themselves. Besides this, in a truly aristocratic household the *laundies,* i.e., the servant girls, were taught singing and dancing, and were called upon to amuse their ladies when they so desired. Besides the music provided by these professional singers and dancers, there was a fund of folk-songs which everybody knew and sang on all occasion. Most of these folk-songs are unfortunately lost now, which is a great pity because, from the ones that remain, it can be seen that they have real literary value. They truly express the sentiments of women — the joy at the birth of a child, the sorrow at the parting from parents, the anguish of saying goodbye to husbands and brothers going to war, the nostalgia for one's own village, the joy of coming home to parents after years of separation, the delight of a brother's visit, the pride when an heir is born in the brother's household — all these are expressed in very simple phrases which touch the heart. These folk-songs are known as *geets,* and no one can hear Amir Khusru's famous farewell *geet* that is sung when a girl says goodbye to her parents, without tears in one's eyes. It is not possible to render into English the lilt and the music and the pathos of these songs. The *sawan* songs that survive are also exponents of similar sentiments of longing for the parents' home and, here again, translation fails to render the sincerity, the pathos and the genuine love that these simple verses give expression to.

Perhaps to western ears this nostalgia for a parents' home in a married woman might seem strange, but to understand it one must remember that girls were married in the East while they were still almost children. Besides this, theirs was not a love marriage; no overriding emotion sweeps them off their feet and makes them joyfully pull out their roots from their childhood surroundings. Theirs was an arranged marriage, and it was years, many years, and sometimes only when their own sons and daughters had grown up and had married in their turn, that a woman began to feel a part and parcel of her husband's house. Until then, her heart keeps

Taoos and *tabla*

constantly flowing back to the home of her father and the friends of her childhood, and the brother who stands as the symbol of all that home meant to her. Therefore, most songs are woven around him, prayers are offered for his long life and pride is taken in his achievements. A child born into a brother's family means the continuity of her father's line and is, therefore, an occasion of joy for her. Tradition also decrees that, on this day, she can claim any treat she likes from her brother, and he cannot deny her request. All this is woven into most appealing verses and lay bare the deep attachment of a sister to the brother, and her pride and reliance on him as a torch bearer of her family.

Another group of folk-songs that were very popular was known as *zacha geeri*. These were sung at the birth of a child, and they expressed the feeling of every member of the family. The mother's joy and feeling of awe at the great responsibility thrust on her, the grandparents' unalloyed pleasure that their line is ensured continuity, the retainers' delight and desire for rewards — these are the thoughts that find expression in songs known as *zacha geeri*. Much of this is lost now; but some of it still lingers on in the memories of those who belong to a past era and one hears them yet, though rarely.

Though music played such an indispensable part in all social events, singing and dancing were relegated, towards the latter period of Moghul civilization, to a certain class only, with the result that girls of good families were not taught singing and dancing as an accomplishment. Ladies of the household who had a good ear or a good voice always picked up a lot of music and sang in informal company and before those of their own age, but they never admitted it openly. It is almost impossible to explain this attitude to Westerners. One has to know so much about the background and the influences to which our society was subjected for this to become comprehensible. Its nearest equivalent in the West can be found in the puritanical attitude of the Quakers. This attitude, although it never succeeded in eliminating music, did have the unfortunate result of relegating this, the highest of the arts, to a class beyond the pale of respectability. The greatest exponents of classical music became the dancing girls known as *tawaifs* These girls were never allowed inside the *zenana;* they performed only before men and on such occasions as weddings and grand banquets; ladies of the household also watched their performance from behind the screen and through latticed windows. *Mujra,* that is singing and dancing by *tawaifs,* was never arranged by, or for, ladies.

A very high degree of proficiency in music was acquired by these *tawaifs,* who were taught vocal and instrumental music from childhood. They took pride in their knowledge of *rag* and *ragni* and were the greatest authority on musical subjects; their position in society, because of this, was a much higher one than it would have been if they were regarded merely as entertainers; they considered themselves as artists and were accepted as such, even though the puritancial section of the society frowned on them and their votaries.

But there was yet another kind of music which always has been, and still is, extremely respectable to listen to — this is the *qawwali*. It can be likened to church music. Actually, these are songs with a religious appeal. At first these were sung only at the shrines of saints. The music is highly emotional and is sung to the accompaniment of several instruments synchronized together. Shrines are still its proper background, and midnight its proper hour; but now it is performed at social gatherings also, generally late in the evening. Orchestra or band music is still unknown in the East; the nearest approach to it is the *shahnai* and the *roshan chowki*. *Shahnai* is a sort of flute played specially at weddings, and *roshan chowki* is a kind of orchestra which was installed for the entire duration of the wedding at the gates of the house. *Takht-e-Ravan* was a sort of portable platform, with musicians and dancing girls sitting on it, that accompanied very grand weddings. In the last twenty-five years I have only heard of one wedding in which the *takht-e-ravan* was a feature, and that was for the heir of the last Nawab of Rampur.

Now with the coming, and the growing popularity, of Western music it appears as if Eastern music will be quite destroyed. I think the Eastern music of the future will be something quite different to the music of the by-gone days, and the tinkle of bells, the jingle of cymbals, and the melody of songs that were heard behind the veil, and which added to the already colourful and somewhat unreal life, and was another element of enchantment, will also become a thing of the past.

And So The Days Went By

XVIII

he reader may well ask what these ladies did when they were not engaged in some ceremony or other for however numerous the ceremonies were, they could not have taken all of their time, nor were their household duties so very arduous, so they must have had a lot of leisure time. Confined behind the veil, what use could they make of it? Poor things! They could not even go shopping, the greatest and the most favoured pastime of women. This is just one other instance that goes to show how little is known of life behind the veil and of social customs in those days.

To begin with, the task of looking after a household consisting not of a few but of dozens of people within itself, was not an easy one. It needed a great deal of tact and wisdom to keep harmony in the home which was, in fact, a miniature world of its own.

The lady of the house enlisted the help of the daughters-in-law and grown-up daughters in the task of supervising and seeing to the comfort of all the members of her household. Within the framework of the family, and inside the four walls of the house, all those people were taken care of who, in a modern society, would be looked after in institutions. An old-fashioned home was an orphanage, a place where the aged and the invalids were taken care of, and one that provided shelter and occupation for destitute gentlewomen without any training for a career. What women now do sitting on committees, those ladies did in their own homes. I think that theirs was the better way, for their charity had warmth and their services were not tinged with patronage. The task of looking after the old and the invalid was given to grown-up girls and that of taking care of orphaned children to young matrons, while the lady of the house herself saw that no one was neglected, and all entrusted to her care had what they needed.

We did not have, and still do not have, old age pensions, homes for the destitute or many orphanages for children, because all such were taken care of in homes themselves. It was unheard of to turn out old servants; and children — not only of relatives but also of neighbours, servants or anyone even remotely connected with the family — if they had lost their parents were taken care of, and brought up according to the station of life to which they belonged.

The lady of the house gave great care to the upbringing of orphaned children because it was considered meritorious to do so. The bringing up of one's own children was one's ordinary duty, but to bring up an orphan was an act that was pleasing to God. And so the education and proper training of orphans was undertaken with great conscientiousness. More thought was given to the

selection of a proper husband for an orphaned girl
under one's care than to the arranging of one's own
daughter's marriage, because a sense of duty was
ingrained in one, and this was part and parcel of a
lady's education.

Ladies behind the veil did a great deal of social
work, only they did not call it so. They called it
doing the work of God, and, therefore, did it with a
sense of humility and not as if they were doing a
favour to those they helped.

Nor did life behind the veil make them unfit to take
part in matters outside the house if they were needed
to do so. Most of them led lives of leisure and were
not called upon to do anything more than surpervise
the household, though as I have tried to say, this in
itself was not an easy task. But very often it
happened that the death of a husband or father
necessitated that ladies supervise the affairs of their
estates and administer vast *jagirs* and, despite the
fact that they were behind the veil, they managed to
do it extremely well. They called in their bailiffs and
managers and spoke to them from behind the veil.
Whenever women had to take charge of their estates,
they proved themselves to be extremely competent.
They checked the books and saw to the minutest
details of administration. If this seems unbelievable,
I would like the reader to remember that not one, but
three successive ladies, ruled the princely state of
Bhopal and every one of them observed the strictest
purdah and each one of them was considered a most
competent ruler. In fact, the last Begum of Bhopal,
was considered the most enlightened among the
rulers of the princely states, and under her
administration Bhopal made great progress. Of

course, this was only possible because our society was so adjusted. It is because our pattern of life was drawn to accept the fact that ladies, being 'behind the veil', missed very little either of the work or the fun of life.

It is true that women did not go shopping, but then, to go to the shops one self, was considered *infra dig* not only for the womenfolk but for the men also if they belonged to the aristocracy or to the gentry. Merchants and shopkeepers brought their wares to the house of milord and milady, and milady did her shopping in her own boudoir, in a leisurely and unhurried manner. When a wedding was on, and before the gala days of *Eid* and *Baqr Eid* there would be a stream of shopkeepers bringing silks and satins, silverware, jewellery, carpets and other articles of household furnishings for milady's inspection. Not only at this time, but all day long women vendors would come bringing lace, ribbons, embroidered silks, and such things which women need — these women were called *bisatan*. Another popular seller of goods was the *chooriwali;* she bought bangles of many varieties and of every colour. Young girls crowded around her box of sparkling wares and she did brisk trade, especially before the gala days. All kinds of snacks and eats were brought around all day long — hot crisp *kachoris* and *jalebies* for breakfast; tasty *kebabs* for a toothsome snack at eleven; ices, iced fruit and *sherbet* in the afternoon. These women sellers also served as a kind of daily newspaper as well, bringing all the gossip of the neighbourhood and serving it together with their wares.

Here the reader may exclaim, 'But how could women go about selling things from door to door if they were in *purdah?*'

The answer to this is that only those women who could afford to remain behind the veil did so and, as it was regarded as a sign of respectability, everyone strove her best to do so as a mark of affluence; but those who could not afford this luxury had to do without it. The women vendors, if they were young, would wear *burqas*, i.e., a sort of veil, but when they became older they would go about with uncovered faces but with *chadars* draped around themselves, carrying their wares on their heads.

For the long winter evenings and summer afternoons, there were many indoors games. Ladies excelled in chess and played cards and many other dice games. Chess was considered quite an accomplishment and had the same place in the social life of those days as bridge has today. Ladies excelled in it, and there are many historic instances where men, having lost heavily at chess, were able to regain their fortune through advice given by their womenfolk on what move to make. But, by far the most popular pastime, and one that still remains as the most popular pastime, is *bait bazi,* this is a kind of poetical contest. Two sides are chosen and each side recites a verse which the other side is supposed to cap by reciting a verse beginning with the last letter the other side's versc has ended with.

Efforts were made to quote verses which had difficult endings like verses ending in the letter *yae* (ے) *yai* (ی) qaf (ق) or *ghain* (غ); contestants would memorize verses ending with one specific letter to exhaust the stock of the opponents, like those ending in *zoai* (ظ) or *zoad* (ض) Both having the *zee* sound but completely different letters in the urdu alphabet.

Sooner or later one side would begin to falter and would begin reciting verses of poor quality or would even start improvising. They were then challenged. The excitement of *bait bazi* can only be appreciated by one who has taken part in it. I would say it was no less exciting than the end of a ball-game.

The person finally unable to recit a verse beginning with the required letter had to accept *math*, i.e., defeat. But in between there was a lot of fun and teasing.

As I have said, knowledge of prosody and versification was considered to be part of a gentleman's education, and women also acquired great proficiency in it. Writing verses and reading them at poetic gatherings called *mushairas* was, therefore, another favourite pastime.

Ladies not only played a number of indoor games but excelled in quite a few outdoor ones as well. This was possible because they had their large walled-off pleasure gardens with swimming pools, etc. They accompanied their menfolk on shooting parties, and took a hand even at big game shooting. I know this sounds incredible, but it is absolutely true, for these ladies had vast estates of their own in which game preserves and shooting boxes were provided; therefore, it was not impossible for them to get plenty of target practice, and many of them took pride in being considered good shots.

In fact, there was time to work and leisure for play. There was none of the hustle and hurry, and none of the stress and strain of modern life. Behind the veil life moved on an even tenor. There was peace and security, gaiety and laughter in it.

And even today, whatever colour there is, whatever

is left of gracious living, of charm of manner and dignity of bearing, is to be found in life 'behind the veil'.